MINISTRY
NUTS AND BOLTS

SECOND EDITION

What They Don't Teach Pastors in Seminary

Aubrey Malphurs

Kregel
Academic & Professional

The Library of Congress has catalogued the first edition as follows:

Library of Congress Cataloging-in-Publication Data
Malphurs, Aubrey.
  Ministry nuts and bolts: what they don't teach pastors in seminary / Aubrey Malphurs.
    p.   cm.
  Includes bibliographical references and index.
  1. Pastoral theology. 2. Clergy—Office. I. Title.
BV4011.M37   1997   253—dc21   97-41092
                                                  CIP
ISBN 978-0-8254-3358-0

Printed in the United States of America

09 10 11 12 13 / 5 4 3 2 1

Contents

121349

List of Figures and Charts

Introduction

Pastor Andrew Johnston was well into his third year at Lake Country Church, and things weren't going well. He knew he was in trouble, and if something didn't change fairly soon, he would need to consider another ministry. The church was an average American church, consisting of seventy-five to eighty-five people, and was divided between two groups. The larger group consisted of members approximately the same age as him and his wife, Carolyn, or younger, who joined after he had become pastor. The smaller group was made up of those who were either a little or a lot older than him and who were members before his call to Lake Country. They had all pulled for him as their pastor, but lately they had begun to question his abilities to lead the ministry. Deep within his heart, he knew that something was wrong—perhaps they were right.

One Saturday morning, Andy was relaxing with a cup of coffee at the dining-room table. It was 7:00 AM, and he had just finished reading the morning paper. As the steam swirled upward from his freshly brewed decaffeinated mocha, he began to reflect on his three years at Lake Country Church.

Pastor Andy realized that most of his problems were in four ministry areas. First, he and the board disagreed on a significant number of ministry issues. This hadn't been true at the beginning. When he had first visited the church in view of a call, they had responded very favorably to all his ideas about the church's future ministry. He had spoken of evangelism and discipleship, and all had nodded their heads in approval. They were all for those things. He hadn't realized, though, that they thought that he was going to pursue those goals himself—not get the board as well as the members to model and accomplish them. Their understanding was that they were hiring *him* to do the ministry; however, his understanding was that he was going to train *them* to do the work of the ministry.

This misunderstanding surfaced after his first anniversary at the church. The members on the board had not responded well to his attempts to meet with them privately to train them in personal evangelism. When he brought up their reluctance in a board meeting, one of the deacons looked at him in surprise. "Pastor," he said, "you're the one who's been to seminary, not us. That's why we hired you! We pay you to do the work of the ministry." When Andy asked why they thought this way, another board member responded, "That's the way we've always done things around here!"

Second, the church seemed to be going nowhere. Pastor Andy hadn't noticed this when he had enlisted for his first tour of ministry duty with the church. Now the first image of his church that popped into his mind was that of a crippled ship adrift on the ocean. His church had no direction. Seminary had taught Andy to preach, and that's what he did every Sunday. The tacit assumption was that 95 percent of pastoral ministry was preaching, and the other 5 percent consisted of such things as weddings, funerals, visitation, and board meetings. This arrangement was something that the average preacher learned to put up with.

After a year of preaching, though, the initial excitement of his coming had worn off. He noted that he wasn't getting the same response to his sermons as at the beginning of his ministry. Some members, mostly women, seemed to be listening and occasionally took notes. But most people weren't as responsive, and some sat and fidgeted while others stared out the windows.

It was during this time that Andy first began to wrestle with his feelings of frustration over the ministry. His frustration unleashed a series of questions that seemed to come from nowhere: Is this what church is all about? Is this what I spent three years of my life in seminary preparing to do? The thought of experiencing this for the rest of his life was frightening and depressing. As he thought further about it, other questions formed: What is this church supposed to be doing? Is this what Christ called me to do? And is this what Christ called his church to do—to show up every Sunday and listen to my preaching? He concluded that there had to be more to ministry than this.

Third, not only was the church going nowhere, but the people gave little thought to the church's future. They simply assumed that it would always be there and do what it had always done. One Sunday a guest speaker had asked the people, "When you close your eyes and think about this church five years, ten years, even twenty years from now, what do you see?" Most sat and stared with puzzled expressions on their faces. No one had ever asked such a question. One of the board members brought it up at the next meeting, and most concurred that they had not thought that much about the church's future except that they needed an infusion of youth or there might not be a future.

Fourth, the assumption in seminary was that discipleship took place primarily as the result of the communication of Scripture, whether preaching or teaching (the homileticians urged the former and the academics the latter). Pastor Andy had some exposure to the ministry of Campus Crusade during his schooling, and they had sold him on a one-on-one or small-group-driven model for discipleship, not the pulpit-driven model of seminary.

Like so many other pastors in the twenty-first century, he observed that people didn't faithfully show up every Sunday to hear him preach. He estimated that most attended the worship service about two or three times a month at best. How could he disciple them through a pulpit ministry alone? Also, Andy concluded that if preaching is the key to discipleship, then mediocre preaching wouldn't do. He needed to be good—real good, which admittedly he wasn't.

An analysis of Andy's four primary areas of struggle reveals that his preparation for pastoral ministry had neglected four foundational ministry concepts. These concepts are key to building Christ's church (see Matt. 16:18). The first foundational ministry concept is *core values*. Whenever people don't get along or differ over major ministry decisions in a church—whether it involves a leadership board or a Sunday school class—the problem often lies in the area of their core values. The *why* question that Andy posed to the board gets at a ministry's core values. Whether he's aware of it or not, every pastor has a core-values set. The same is true for the church. And it's these organizational values that drive all that a ministry does. When a pastor and a board hold to different values, they will seldom agree on the direction of the ministry.

The second foundational ministry concept is *mission*. A church's drifting in no particular direction indicates that it doesn't have a clear, compelling ministry direction. It might have gotten by with this in the church-friendly culture of the 1940s and 1950s, but not in the skeptical culture that characterizes the 1990s and beyond. Pastor Andy's *what* question, "What is this church supposed to be doing?" is the mission question. What does the Bible say the church should be doing? That no one in Pastor Andy's church could answer the mission question is a sure sign that the church is in serious trouble. It doesn't know where it's going or what it's supposed to be doing. These are mission issues.

The third foundational ministry concept is *vision*. Vision as well as mission has everything to do with the church's future. It's a mental picture of what the ministry's tomorrow will look like. It's a snapshot of the church's future and all its exciting possibilities. That Pastor Andy's board in particular and the people in general don't have a vision is not a good sign. While this church isn't entirely aware of it, it's in serious trouble. Business as usual will not suffice in the information age when change is a constant. A church that is without a clear vision of its future places that future in jeopardy. It desperately needs a preferred future. Instead, it harbors a museum mentality; it mirrors church life and leadership in a bygone era.

The fourth foundational ministry concept is *strategy*. Every church has a strategy. It may be a good one or a bad one. The latter is the situation at Lake Country. One reason their strategy is bad is because strategies exist to implement missions, and Lake Country doesn't have a mission. Another reason is that the present strategy is based on some past mission that has long since been lost and forgotten. A third is that the present strategy simply isn't working. That strategy mirrors an outdated three-to-thrive mentality that consists of three meetings a week: a Sunday morning service including a Sunday school, a Sunday evening service, and a Wednesday night prayer meeting.

The people's expectations for all these meetings are that the pastor will preach a sermon or at least teach a Bible lesson. Pastor Andy has been faithful to those expectations. The people, though, also "vote with their feet." While an interest in prayer exists, only a handful of faithful old-timers show up for Wednesday night prayer meeting. Also, Sunday night attendance has dropped dramatically over the past ten years to the point that Pastor Andy wonders if they should cancel the meeting. So far they continue to meet because he enjoys teaching the Bible on Sunday nights, and the board members believe that to cancel Sunday night church sends the wrong message to the people.

Of the church's three meetings, most people will attend the Sunday morning worship service. Their attendance fluctuates, on average, between two and three times a month. If people can be discipled from the pulpit alone, which is doubtful, then two or three sermons a month aren't sufficient to make disciples. Actually, most congregants at Lake Country aren't sure what a disciple is. If you asked, they'd confess that they wouldn't know what a disciple looks like even if one walked through the front door of the church.

The tragedy of all these problems is twofold. First, Lake Country's problems go beyond this small church. These problems are faced by a significant number of older churches all across North America—churches that are in deep trouble. In what has become a predominantly secular culture, small churches are becoming a thing of the past. Lyle Schaller summarizes it best when he writes that "two-thirds to three-fourths of all congregations founded before 1960 are either on a plateau in size or shrinking in number."[1]

Second, Pastor Andy completed the typical basic training for pastors at a very fine evangelical institution. He graduated near the top of his class with the assumption that he was prepared to pastor a church. He has learned the hard way, however, that he wasn't. The idea that pastoral ministry is to be equated with the pulpit is fallacious and unbiblical. A quick survey of the Epistles reveals that Paul, and others who often functioned in pastoral roles, spent as much time evangelizing the lost as they did preaching to and teaching the saved. While this assumption worked to some extent in a sympathetic, churched culture of the past, it doesn't in the unsympathetic, unchurched culture in which pastors find themselves today. As they say in the South, "That dog won't hunt." Unfortunately for seminary graduates, many of our classical evangelical seminaries appear to have missed the paradigm shift that has taken place in our culture. Instead, they are preparing pastors to minister as if we are still living back in the 1940s and 1950s.

This isn't to argue that preaching and teaching the Bible aren't important. Nothing could be further from the truth. The proclamation of God's Word is central and essential to any ministry because Scripture is truth (John 17:17), and today's lost and dying generation desperately needs to hear biblical truth. Ministry, though, must not be primarily equated with the communication of biblical truth from a pulpit in a sanctuary or a podium in a classroom.

Neither is a pastor to be solely equated with a preacher. If the typical church's difficult days of the 1980s and 1990s have taught us anything, it's that the pastor needs to be a leader and a coach of leaders as well as a preacher. Yet a perusal of the catalogs of many of our best evangelical schools reveals that only one or, at the most, two courses are offered on leadership. In spite of the fact that every church survives on the basis of competent lay leadership, future pastors graduate not knowing how to recruit and train these leaders.

Those who would lead and pastor the newer paradigm churches of the twenty-first century have a new imperative. They must think about vital leadership and ministry concepts such as core values, mission, vision, and strategy as well as how they relate to one another (see fig. I.1). These concepts make up the ministry ABCs. While there are other ministry ABCs (character development, stewardship, and so forth), these basic concepts form the fundamental nuts and bolts of any ministry. The evangelical churches that God is blessing in North America have carefully thought through these concepts and positioned themselves accordingly. Thus, it behooves the rest of the churches to learn from their examples and pursue the same if the future church is to have maximum impact for the Savior in the third millennium.

I have written this book to help leaders, pastors, and church boards think through these ministry ABCs. Part 1 consists of three chapters that will help leaders understand, discover, and develop their own *core values* as well as those that drive their ministries. Part 2 presents two chapters on defining and then developing a *mission* for ministry. Part 3 provides three chapters on the *vision* concept. Chapter 6 defines a ministry vision, while chapter 7 distinguishes the vision from a mission. Chapter 8 will assist leaders in developing a *vision* statement for their ministries. Part 4 consists of two chapters on defining and then developing a strategy that is tailor-made for each ministry.

I have included discussion questions designed to help individual leaders grasp and apply the ideas in each chapter. I recommend that pastors and board members read this book together and discuss the ideas as a group. The questions will help leaders raise as well as wrestle with the tough issues that some might otherwise avoid.

Figure I.1. Leadership and Ministry Concepts

Part 1

The Values of Your Ministry

1

The Definition of Core Values

What Is a Credo?

A vital element of pastoral leadership today is to make sure that the ministry organization knows itself. Certain durable core values or beliefs underlie and define every organization—whether it's a church, a parachurch ministry, or a marketplace entity. Core values are fundamental to all that the organization does. They are ministry defining and have everything to do with a ministry's distinctiveness. They are what distinguishes one ministry from another, and they explain why some people are attracted to your church while others are repelled. They dictate personal involvement. If an individual's core values align with the ministry's, that individual is more likely to invest his or her life in that ministry. Values communicate what is important—the organization's bottom line. Thus, core values define what you believe is God's heart for your ministry or church.

Values are responsible for a number of other things as well. They not only inspire people to ministry, but they also enhance your leadership as well as shape the very character of your ministry. Most often, values are key to a church's success or failure. Consequently, to say that discovering and establishing core values is important might be an understatement—they are critical to the existence of your ministry. In *Rediscovering Church*, pastor Bill Hybels writes, "In fact, establishing the core principles is so important that I'll be devoting an entire chapter to the values that Willow Creek's leaders have identified as central to accomplishing our mission."[1] Unfortunately for Andy and the church, no one has ever instructed them in the importance of the ministry basics, or in this case, the importance of identifying and understanding their essential values.

Since a ministry's core values are so important, we must pursue the question, *What are core organizational values?* The purpose of this chapter is to answer that question. I will begin by defining what core values aren't. Next, I will provide a foundational working definition of what they are. Finally, I'll build on that foundation by examining the various kinds of values.

WHAT CORE VALUES ARE NOT

Those who write on leadership and the organizational basics often confuse values with other key concepts. This makes it difficult for ministry leaders who desire to identify and work with these concepts. I draw a sharp line between the God-honoring values and the mission, vision, strategy, and doctrinal statements of a ministry.

Values Are Not a Mission

First, do not make the mistake of equating your set of core ministry values with your ministry mission. As you'll discover in part 2 of this book, your ministry mission is a statement of what your ministry is supposed to accomplish. Your core values are not the same as your mission. Core values answer the *why* question for your ministry. They explain why you do what you do, supplying the God-ordained reasons behind what you do. They not only shape your congregational culture but dictate the precise biblical mission that you choose for your ministry.

Values Are Not a Vision

Second, do not confuse your core ministry values with your ministry vision. Like the mission, your vision also addresses what your ministry is, according to the Bible, supposed to be doing. Whereas the mission states in one sentence what you plan to accomplish, the vision paints a picture of the same. And whereas the mission involves the hill your army needs to take, the vision is what your army will look like on top of the hill.

Your ministry values should differ from your vision in at least three fundamental ways. First, like your ministry mission, the vision also answers the *what* question. It provides a clear snapshot of what the church is supposed to be doing. The central values answer the *why* question, providing the reasons for your vision.

Second, contrary to what many believe, a church isn't vision driven. It is *values* driven and vision focused. On the one hand, when a ministry takes the time to carefully articulate its vision, its future comes into focus. The people who make up that ministry are better able to see the future; they can envision what they're supposed to be doing. On the other hand, when a ministry has a shared set of values, it knows what is driving that ministry. Values move the ministry. They are the hidden motivators that dictate every decision it makes, every problem it solves, and every dollar it spends.

Third, every ministry, whether church or parachurch, has a set of core values. The ministry may or may not be aware of those values, and the values may be good or bad. Regardless, a values set is present because something drives the ministry. One of the reasons, though, that so many churches sprinkled across North America today are in trouble is because they have neither a vision nor a mission. They haven't given much thought to what their future looks like; consequently, their future looks grim.

Values Are Not a Strategy

Third, you will confuse those in your ministry if you equate your values with your strategy. While your core values answer the *why* question, your strategy answers the *how* question. Values dictate the mission you choose for your ministry. Values will also determine the strategy that you select to implement that mission in your ministry community. Your strategy, though, addresses how you will realize your mission. The early church, for example, adopted Christ's Great Commission mandate (Matt. 28:19; Mark 16:15) as their *mission* statement (Acts 1:8). Their *strategy* for realizing this mission consisted primarily of the three missionary journeys that Luke recorded in Acts 13–14; 15:36–18:22; and 18:23–21:16. The biblical *values* that surfaced in ministries such as the church at Jerusalem (Acts 2:42–47) deeply influenced this strategy.

Values Are Not a Doctrinal Statement

Fourth, many leaders and laypeople confuse the sound set of core values with that of the doctrinal statement of theological beliefs. When I conduct a seminar on developing a statement of values, called a credo, people often raise their hands and ask if I'm talking about developing a doctrinal statement for their churches. My answer is an emphatic, "No!" Most have a doctrinal statement; few, if any, have a credo or statement of core values.

The credo is the key precept that drives the ministry and dictates what its mission, vision, and strategy will be. A church's doctrinal statement is a written document of its collected theological beliefs regarding such vital concepts as God, the Bible, the Trinity, Christ, the Holy Spirit, man, sin, angels, salvation, the church and its future state. Some slight overlap could exist between a credo and doctrinal statement, such as the importance of the Scriptures in directing the ministry or the Great Commission as the church's mission. When comparing a church's credo with its doctrinal statement, however, the difference is obvious. Consequently, I've provided an example of one church's credo and its doctrinal statement in appendix A. Compare the two and you'll quickly discern the differences.

WHAT CORE VALUES ARE

Now that you understand what core values are not, I'll define what they are. I define a Christian organization's values as the constant, passionate, biblical core beliefs that drive the ministry (see fig. 1.1). Core values are defined by five vital characteristics.

Core Values Are Constant

In the past, some old-timers caustically stated that the only thing you can be sure of is death and taxes. Today, we must add change. Secular writers tell us that change is now a constant—and they're right. North America is in transition from the modern to the postmodern era. Whenever any country drifts from one era into another, it passes through a white-water change that affects the social, economic, political, and technological dynamics of that country.

The question for the church is *How will it choose to respond to this accelerating change?* In the 1950s and 1960s, it chose to ignore it. The typical church of that period functioned at a pace that was from five to twenty years behind our culture. Consequently, many a church has been out of touch with the people as well as the technology that could help it conduct its ministry more efficiently. Some churches are convinced that the computer is a tool of the Antichrist, and that a mimeograph and stencil is preferable to a copier.

The key to dealing with change is determining what will help the church versus what will hurt it. But how can churches do this? One way is to discover and articulate your ministry's fundamental hierarchy of values. In Acts 2:42–47, Luke reveals that the Jerusalem church understood its values (see appendix B). This understanding helped them navigate their ministry ship through the sea of change that was taking place all around them as they struggled to move from an era of law to an era of grace. It also helped the Twelve in Acts 6:1–7 determine and focus their ministry (prayer and the ministry of the Word) during a turbulent time when they could have drifted off course.

If a ministry's core values are to guide it through difficult times of transition, those values must not be in transition. If the values drive the ministry and if they change every other year, then the ministry will constantly be changing courses. The result will be chaos. At one moment the church targets the believing community, consisting of the already convinced. The next moment, the church has decided to change course and target unchurched lost people—the unconvinced. This leaves followers confused, bewildered, and angry.

Throughout a leader's growth and development, as well as that of his or her ministry, there will be times of transition during which values formation takes place. An example is when a leader, such as Pastor Andy, has attended a university or theological seminary. Andy left seminary with some values that he didn't have when he matriculated. He also jettisoned a few. As he continues to stretch and grow as a leader, he will continue to adopt new values and drop others. To a certain extent, Andy and most pastors constantly define and hone the unique set of values that undergird their ministries—here a tweak and there a tweak. It's imperative, however, that they reach a point in their ministry development when those beliefs don't change appreciably.

Another period of transition for the leader is a ministry-paradigm shift. The older, preboomer generation of North American pastors are facing this dilemma. They were trained under an older paradigm for ministry that was primarily pulpit driven. People also followed their leadership simply because of the authority of their positions—congregants did what the pastor asked because he was the pastor.

Core Values Are Passionate

Whereas vision is a "seeing" word, passion is a "feeling" word. Leaders feel passionately about their core values. Every leader has numerous values, but they are passionate about only a few. Your intellect will tell you what your values are, and if you conduct a values inventory, you might list fifty to one hundred values. Your heart, though, will tell you which of those values are priority—which ones you are passionate about.

Core values do more than build a fire in your heart and stir your emotions. They move you to action. You can't walk away from your core values unmoved, or they aren't core values. Core values are infectious. They leave you with a sense that you must do something about them. They move or drive you toward the vision—from what *is* to what ought to be. If I value authentic biblical community, then I'll be in some sort of small group. If I value prayer, then I'll frequently be on my knees. If lost people matter to me, then I'll spend time with them. If evangelism is at my core, then I'll become a contagious Christian.

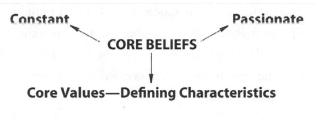

Figure 1.1. Core Values—Defining Characteristics

Core Values Are Biblical

The core values that make up a ministry's credo should be Bible based. If you look through the credos in appendix B, you will note that several actually provide biblical references. Saddleback Valley Community Church of Mission Viejo, California, lists seventeen core values. Every value has at least one passage of Scripture, some have two or three, and one has five. Other churches may not quote or reference a passage of Scripture but the values are obviously Bible based. Willow Creek Community Church of Barrington, Illinois, states, "We believe that lost people matter to God, and, therefore, ought to matter to us." Though they provide no biblical text, such passages as Luke 15 and Luke 19:1–10 prove the point.

Some values don't appear to have scriptural warrant. You read them and wonder what the biblical basis might be. But must every value in a credo be biblically based? There is a significant difference in the words *should be* and *must be*. On the one hand, I prefer that there be a biblical text for every belief. The true test of a core value is, *Is it scriptural?* If there is no biblical basis, then perhaps it's not biblical. On the other hand, I believe that all truth is God's truth and that, while all the content of the Bible is true (John 17:17), not all truth is found in the Bible. It is true, for instance, that one plus one equals two, yet I don't find that in my Bible. How, then, can we know if something is true when it's not found in the Bible? Scientific evidence is not always reliable. The best scientific minds once believed that the earth, not the sun, was the center of the solar system. I believe it's possible to have values based on God's truth that isn't found in the Scriptures. Non-scripturally based values, though, are more characteristic of for-profit marketplace organizations such as health facilities, retail stores, grocery stores, and restaurants than of decidedly Christian ministries that are nonprofit organizations.

Core Values Are Core Beliefs

Two characteristics of core values are that they are *core* and that they are *beliefs*. First, they are core. If you were to list all your organizational values, the list would be long, depending on the time you take to perform this task. The more time you take, the longer the list. I have looked through the values found in the sample credos in my book *Values-Driven Leadership*, first or second editions, and discovered that there are around one hundred values, though some are almost the same but worded differently. All these values are important because they affect your ministry organization in some way. Some values, however, influence your church more than do others. If you returned to your list of values, most likely you would find the more important values listed first with the least important values listed toward the end. Your most important values are those that are at the core. They are essential to what you do. They dictate what you believe is God's heart for your ministry and are found at the top of your priority list.

Second, your core values are your beliefs. As I said earlier in this chapter, core values aren't, though, the kinds of beliefs that are found in a doctrinal statement. Core values are not representative of the church's theological beliefs, though core values are based on theology. The deity of the Holy Spirit and one's view of the end times are central beliefs to the theology of any church, but these beliefs probably won't be the core values that drive the church.

Some synonyms for your core values are *convictions, precepts, ideals, standards,* and *assumptions.* Core values are the organization's fundamental set of convictions on which it premises all of its actions and policies. They are the deep, intrinsic precepts that define your ministry organization. They mirror the essence of your ministry and what you will accomplish as the result of holding to them. If you examine them carefully, you'll see that they are the primary hidden motivators of your entire church or parachurch ministry. If you review the values of the Jerusalem church either in Acts 2:42–47 or appendix B against the backdrop of the entire book of Acts, you will quickly discover that they define the very heart of the church. They explain why the church accomplished what it accomplished in the book of Acts and beyond.

Core Values Drive Your Ministry

Your church's core values move the ministry in a particular, unique direction. Earlier in this chapter, I stated that every ministry is vision focused and values driven. Values sit in the driver's seat of your ministry vehicle. They quietly (and sometimes not so quietly) drive the ministry in a particular direction. An understanding of your core values explains your ministry's behavior and why it behaves the way it does. They affect most everything you do—decision making, problem solving, risk taking, goal setting, team building, and financial spending.

KINDS OF VALUES

To gain a clear understanding of core values, we have looked at what they aren't and then defined what they are. We can accrue additional understanding by examining the different kinds of values.

Conscious Versus Unconscious Values

The core values of a Christian ministry exist at a conscious or unconscious level. As I conduct seminars and consult with ministry organizations, I find that most hold their values at an unconscious level. That's one reason why I often refer to them as hidden motivators. Like Pastor Andy and the board at Lake Country Church, people have ministry-defining precepts but aren't completely aware of what they are or the impact those precepts exert on their ministries.

Consequently, it becomes the leaders' responsibility to discover and communicate the values of their churches. By moving values from the unconscious to the conscious level, all will essentially know why they are doing what they are doing. If some people hold to certain unbiblical standards, they will know what they are and have the opportunity to change them. If church leaders find themselves in constant disagreement, they'll know precisely where the problems lie.

The Jerusalem church seems to have been conscious of its core values. Otherwise, Luke might not have been able to articulate them as he did in Acts 2:42–47. In verse 42 he says that "they devoted themselves to" their values. They knew them at a conscious level because they lived them at a conscious level.

Shared Versus Unshared Values

Common cause is essential to accomplishing all that Christ has called us to do. Common cause starts with shared values. Without question, the reason that the early church was so effective is because of its shared values. If Pastor Andy and his board were to identify the values that are driving their decisions, they would find that most of those values are not shared.

Had they known this before the church's marriage to Andy as its pastor, it would have saved all of them much grief. If a ministry board is to work together, it must share to a great degree its core values.

Kouzes and Posner conducted research that involved over 2,300 managers at varying levels and discovered that shared values

- foster strong feelings of personal effectiveness;
- promote high levels of company loyalty;
- facilitate consensus about key organization goals and stakeholders;
- encourage ethical behavior;
- promote strong norms about working hard and caring;
- reduce levels of job stress and tension.[7]

While it is doubtful that Kouzes and Posner included any Christian ministries in their survey, certainly church and parachurch ministries could realize these same results.

Many American churches at the dawn of the twenty-first century find themselves in a struggle for survival. A common characteristic of this struggle for survival is sagging attendance. One solution that a number of churches have pursued is to merge—by joining forces their chances of survival are much better. On the surface this seems to make good sense; however, I know of few mergers that have worked. Most often they either split, or one of the merged parties eventually disperses to other churches. While there are numerous reasons why mergers tend to fail, a primary factor is unshared values.

Christians who hold to common values feel empowered to accomplish a mission, are intensely loyal to a cause, feel a deeper sense of effectiveness, work harder, and most importantly, they care deeply about one another and want to minister together. According to Acts 4:32, Luke writes that the Jerusalem church had achieved common cause: "All the believers were one in heart and mind." Acts 2:42–47 would seem to indicate that a major cause for this was shared values.

Personal Versus Organizational Values

Your core values exist on two levels—the personal and the organizational. People who make up a church or parachurch organization will have a values set, whether on a conscious or unconscious level, that they bring to their ministry. These are their personal, individual, or private values.

Aspiring church planters would be wise to discover their personal values before they begin a church because their private values will naturally become the organization's public values. When such values are articulated by the church planter, people who share them might be inclined to either join the church or support it financially. People who differ at the values level will look for another church. This approach benefits all parties and eliminates potential problems before they have a chance to develop.

Those who desire to lead an established church, such as Pastor Andy, would also be wise to discover their own personal values first. With these firmly in mind, they are ready to look for a ministry with similar values. This makes for a ministry match that won't result in a divorce after a year or two. I recommend that a pastor and church agree on at least 60 percent of the values before they go to the altar. Anything less places the so-called marriage in serious jeopardy from the start. Not only is agreeing on 60 percent of the values important, but the values they agree upon are also key. A vital example is evangelism. A church that doesn't value evangelism is in deep trouble and will find itself in decline, if it's not already.

Every organization, Christian or secular, has a set of defining precepts. I refer to these as organizational, institutional, or corporate values. I use the word *institution* as a synonym for an organization. I also use the word *corporation* as a synonym for a ministry organization, though it emphasizes the organization as a legal entity. It is correct to use the word *corporation* of the church especially if it has incorporated.

Not only should pastors as leaders examine their core values, they should be able to articulate their credos, and churches should do the same. I recommend that every church have a published credo such as those in appendix B. It will help the church differentiate between their good and bad values so that they can pour their efforts into the former while trying to correct the latter. A published credo will help potential members determine whether they should join this ministry or look for another. It also will assist the church in the selection of a pastor as well as other primary leaders, whose personal values must be in reasonable alignment with the church's.

Actual Versus Aspirational Values

All leaders, as well as their organizations, have both actual and aspirational values. Actual values are those that you own and act upon daily in your ministry. At some time in your life, you have embraced them, and now they are a part of you. They are intuitive, and they naturally manifest themselves as you lead your ministry. When you have to make an organizational decision, values automatically spring into action—whether or not you're aware of them.

Aspirational values are those that you or your ministry doesn't own but would like to. Therefore, you don't normally act upon them unless you make a concentrated effort to do so. While actual values represent what is true about you, aspirational values represent what might or could be true about you. My experience has taught me that most pastors do not have the gift of evangelism, and they do not consistently share their faith. This is especially true of seminary graduates who pastor the smaller churches in North America. While all will vote for evangelism, that they aren't doing evangelism on a consistent basis proves that it exists more as an aspirational value than as an actual value.

How can you know which values are actual and which are aspirational? The simple test is to observe your behavior or that of your ministry. If, for example, evangelism is taking place on a consistent basis, you own that value—it is actual. If not, then it is aspirational. We know that the Jerusalem church's values were actual because Luke writes in Acts 2:42 that "they devoted themselves to the apostles' teaching . . . the fellowship . . . the breaking of bread . . . prayer." In short, they practiced what they believed.

Understanding this distinction is important when you attempt to discover and articulate your personal credo or that of your ministry. What you want to discover are your actual values, not your aspirational values. You want to list what is really true of your ministry, not what you hope is true or want to be true in the future. Should you make the mistake of mixing both true and desired values in your credo, then those who observe your ministry will question your integrity. If you say that you value prayer but rarely pray, then you are acting hypocritically.

This raises the question, *What do we do with our aspirational values?* What if you're a seminary graduate and the pastor of a small church, who wants to embrace evangelism as a core value? What if you are attempting to share your faith with the lost on a consistent basis? Aspirational values become part of the *mission* and *strategy* of the ministry. They are the things toward which the ministry is striving. They can be listed in a statement separate from the values-based credo, as a list of values that the church does not yet own but is working toward.

Single Versus Multiple Values

All ministry organizations as well as leaders have multiple values. If you took time out of your life to list them, they could range from fifty to one hundred and fifty. Again, the core or essential values are those at the top of the list. Some ministries, however, have a single, all-encompassing value that tends to dwarf all the others in the credo.

This is true of your ministry if (1) there is quite a distance between the first-listed value and all the rest, and (2) when you ask people what first comes to mind when they think about your ministry, they consistently allude to a single value such as worship, evangelism, or Bible teaching. Then you know you have a predominate controlling value.

Chart 1.1 presents several single values that characterize a number of churches that minister on the North American scene. One is the classroom church whose overriding value is information or, to be more precise, Bible

Type of Church	Unifying Value	Role of Pastor	Role of People	Key Emphasis	Typical Tool	Desired Result	Source of Legitimacy	Positive Trait
The Classroom Church	Information	Teacher	Student	To know	Overhead projector	Educated Christian	Expository preaching	Knowledge of Bible
The Soul-winning Church	Evangelism	Evangelist	Bringer	To save	Altar call	Born-again people	Numbers	Heart for lost
The Social-Conscience Church	Justice	Reformer	Recruiter	To care	Petition	Activist	Cause	Compassion for oppressed
The Experiential Church	Experience	Performer	Audience	To feel	Handheld mike	Empowered Christian	Spirit	Vitality
The Family-Reunion Church	Loyalty	Chaplain	Siblings	To belong	Potluck	Secure Christian	Roots	Identity
The Life-Development Church	Character	Coach	Ministry	To be	Ephesians 4	Disciple	Changed lives	Growth

Chart 1.1. Types of American Evangelical Churches

content. When people think about attending the classroom church, their thoughts primarily focus on biblical content. They are drawn to these teaching churches because they want to learn more about the Scriptures.

The critical question is: Are single-value churches good or bad? Is it a good idea to have one overarching value or better to have a balance of beliefs? I believe the issue is one of biblical balance. God's people need to consume a balanced spiritual diet. To live on dessert alone is not healthy. The problem with the teaching church is that far too often evangelism rarely takes place. And the problem with the evangelistic church is that little teaching takes place. Both, however, fall under the church's mission according to the Great Commission (Matt. 28:19–20).

What alternative is there for those who attend a single-value church? To gain a balanced diet, they would need to attend a variety of churches rather than a single church. Last Sunday they might have attended First Community Church. This Sunday they may attend Second Community Church, and next Sunday they perhaps plan to attend Third Community. This sounds strangely like a three-ring circus and is not a viable biblical option. The solution is for the single-value church to move quickly toward a healthy, balanced approach.

Conscious	vs.	Unconscious
Shared	vs.	Unshared
Personal	vs.	Organizational
Actual	vs.	Aspirational
Single	vs.	Multiple
Congruent	vs.	Incongruent
Good	vs.	Bad

Chart 1.2. Kinds of Values

QUESTIONS FOR REFLECTION, DISCUSSION, AND APPLICATION

1. If you are a pastor, do you and your board disagree on many issues? If you are a board member, do you disagree a lot with your pastor? If you answered yes to either question, how would you explain your disagreements? What do you plan to do about this?

2. Are you convinced that your core values are important? Other than those mentioned in this book, can you think of other reasons why core values are important? If yes, what are those reasons?

3. What is the difference between your values and your mission? Your vision? Your strategy? Your doctrinal statement? Have you confused any of these?

4. As you examine your core values, have they remained constant over the years? Have any changed? If they have, when? Do you anticipate changes in the future?

5. What, if anything, are you passionate about? What does passion have to do with your personal values?

6. Are your core values biblical? Can you cite a passage of Scripture that supports your values? If not, why not?

7. Do your values drive your ministry? If so, how? What kind of impact do they exert on your decisions, goals, finances? Prior to reading this book, were you aware of your values and how they affect your ministry?

8. Are most of your values or those of your ministry held at a conscious or unconscious level? Do you and your board share many values? How has this sharing or lack thereof affected you and the ministry?

9. Are your values mostly aspirational or actual? What's the difference? Do you sense that a single value predominates your church? If so, what is it? Do you suspect that either you or your ministry has some bad values? Name one.

2

The Discovery of Core Values

What Is Your Credo?

The focus of part 1 of this book is the discovery of personal and corporate values. Leaders, whether professional staff or lay board members, have their own set of core organizational values. Leaders will greatly enhance their ministries and save themselves much pain if they discover and articulate their personal values first. The preparation of leaders—whether in churches, Bible or Christian colleges, and seminaries—should include the discovery and formation of each leader's set of fundamental values.

The ministry itself will have a corporate values set. The church or parachurch organization should discover and communicate through a credo the values that drive it as a ministry. A credo serves to define the ministry of a church and communicate to all what it's about, providing the ministry's distinctive "up front" so that potential members may determine if a particular church is the place for them. The organizations or subministries such as Christian education, worship, and so on that make up the broader ministry will also have organizational values. Subministry values must be congruent and under the umbrella of the organization's values set. If, for example, the church values creativity and innovation, then the subministries should value the same.

Suppose the seminary that Andy attended had carefully taught its pastoral students the ministry ABCs, including the concept of core organizational values. Assume that a required course had taught all aspiring pastors to discover their values and then had taught them how to discover those of their prospective churches. What would that course be like? The values-discovery process consists of at least three steps: (1) determining who discovers the ministry's values; (2) deciding or discovering which values to unearth (using the values audit); (3) learning how to resolve values differences.

WHO DISCOVERS THE MINISTRY'S VALUES?

The first step is to determine who is involved in the discovery process. The ideal is to have everyone who is associated with the ministry involved. Since this isn't feasible, the responsibility rests with the primary leadership. In the church, this would be the head pastor, any staff, and the church board. In the parachurch ministry, this would be a president or general director, and the ministry board. In the marketplace, it would be the president, CEO, and the corporate board.

Most people, even good leaders, desire to be led in some way. Regardless of the environment—spiritual, military, or political—people look for leaders with character. They look for men and women who cast a significant vision for their people and define what's really important to the establishment. One of the important contributions that leaders make to their organizations is to discover, communicate, implement, and enforce the central corporate beliefs. Regardless of who actually discovers the values, the leadership is responsible to see that values discovery takes place.

Although primary leaders are responsible for discovering values, they must not attempt the process alone. A characteristic of a great leader is to involve others in the action. If the organization is a church, then the size of the church will dictate who is involved and to what degree (see fig. 2.1). The sheer size of a large church means that a smaller percentage, in relation to total active workers, is involved in the values-discovery process. This would include those on the staff and board along with lay leaders of certain vital ministries in the church. People who serve in large churches sense that due to the ministry's size not everyone can have his or her say. Consequently, those who serve are more dependent on those at a higher level of leadership.

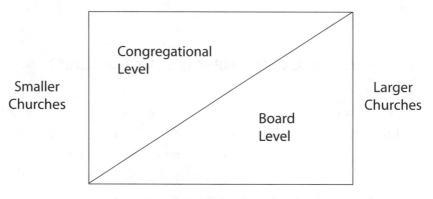

Figure 2.1. Levels of Involvement

In a smaller church, a larger percentage of those who serve may take an active part in the process, beginning with the pastor and the board and including other leaders ranging from Sunday school teachers to small-group leaders. At Lake Country Church, this would comprise Pastor Andy, his board, input from the Sunday school teachers, and a few other key people. The problem in the smaller church is that the "squeaky wheels" who often represent special interests have a louder voice than in a larger ministry. Consequently, it takes strong, skillful leadership to protect the church from the undue influence of these voices.

HOW DO YOU DECIDE OR DISCOVER THE MINISTRY'S VALUES?

The way that you discover your ministry organization's core values is by conducting a values audit. Its purpose is not to create or shape the values but to discover those, whether good or bad, that are already in place and currently driving the ministry. Thus, the focus is on actual not aspirational values. Should the ministry mistakenly articulate its aspirational values, then its people will question the credibility of the institution and its leadership. They will examine the value and protest, "We don't believe that!"

Since a ministry's defining values exist at two levels—the personal and the congregational—you will need to audit both levels. It is best that you start with your personal values, then move to the values of the ministry institution that you serve or hope to serve. This exercise is mandatory for church boards as well as for pastors and their staffs. The same is true for those in similar positions in parachurch ministries. Students preparing for ministry should discover not only their personal core values but also know how to unearth those of a prospective ministry.

Auditing Personal Values

Several ways exist for you to audit your personal values. You may pursue one or, even better, a combination of the following.

Write them down on a piece of paper. The assumption is that you know what a value is. If not, then look briefly at a sample credo or two in appendix B. I use the term *briefly* because you don't want another organization's credo to unduly influence the process. Initially, you may write several sentences in an attempt to capture the value. The goal, however, is brevity because brevity leads to clarity. The simplest approach is to write a statement such as "I value relevant Bible exposition." The temptation will be to say much more. Instead, use the shortened form: I value _____.

If you must say more, then place your explanation below the initial value statement. The credo of Lakeview Community Church of Cedar Hill, Texas, provides an example of how to do this (see appendix B).

Review the credos of several churches, looking for a common cause. For example, you might look over the values in the credos found in appendix B.[1] Some values will figuratively jump off the page at you—they are your personal values. You will feel an affinity with them. They will attract your attention, and you will experience a sense of common cause. Write these down. You must focus on your actual values as well as your aspirational values. At this point in the process, the purpose of the audit is to discover what you believe, not what you should believe.

Take the Personal Core Values Audit in appendix C. This audit focuses more on a church but includes some parachurch organizations. As you and those in your ministry look over the beliefs listed in this audit, certain ones should grab your attention. Again, as in the paragraph above, you will feel an affinity with some but not with others. Rate the values in importance to you from 1 (the lowest) to 4 (the highest). There is also a place for you to add any values that you might own that aren't on the list. The ones you've rated as a 4 are your core values. Prioritize those with the highest scores, and choose the top six.

Auditing Corporate Values

Several techniques are available for auditing a church or parachurch ministry's core organizational values. The first three will help prospective leaders know in advance a ministry's values if they are not articulated or known. The third and fourth will help a ministry discover its own values.

Request that the ministry provide a copy of its credo. Do this if you aspire to serve the ministry in some way as leader, staff, or volunteer. One of the reasons I wrote *Values-Driven Leadership* was to call attention to the need for ministries to discover and articulate their God-honoring values. I have observed that more ministries are developing credos. It shouldn't surprise you, however, if the ministry you're interested in doesn't have one or doesn't even know what you're requesting. This is still a relatively new concept, though it's a ministry basic.

Articulate a ministry's values based on your personal observation. This requires that you visit the ministry or have some involvement in it. When, for example, you attend a church service, you can discern a number of the church's values by skillful observation. When you approach the church, you should note if the facilities are well maintained and if the grounds are properly kept. Once inside the facility, are there signs of poor maintenance? Is there a sense of excitement and enthusiasm among the attendees? Is the worship planned and performed well? What is the sermon about and did people respond? If it's a Baptist church, inquire about the number of baptisms—you'll get a feel for its passion toward evangelism.

Use the Church Ministry Core Values Audit in appendix D. I have designed this audit to help ministries in general but churches in particular to unearth their values. It will accomplish the same for those who desire to know a ministry's values before identifying with the organization. Lake Country Church could have used it to discover their values in order to list them in a church credo. They could have then mailed their credo to potential pastor Andy before any courtship. Had he known, Pastor Andy could have used this audit during their engagement to determine if there should have been a marriage with Lake Country Church. Their not having done this, both Andy and the church are now facing the possibility of a painful divorce. Every leader and every ministry should use their courtship as a time to discern their values alignment.

Gather the ministry team and discover common values together. While gathering the entire team is preferable, it's also possible to gather different groups in the organization on different days. This works for both large and small ministries. CAM International, an independent missions organization located in Dallas, Texas, used this process at one of their annual convocations, which involved approximately 250 missionaries.

Begin the process by breaking the organization up into work teams of five to ten people. Either assign or ask each team to determine a leader to facilitate discussion and a recorder to take notes. Ask each group to brainstorm and determine what they believe are the ministry's key driving values. They may list as many as they want. You might show them several examples to help catalyze the process. Remind them that a good value is biblical, passionate, shared, constant, clear, implementable, and congruent with all the other values.

Once the groups have composed their lists, require them to eliminate all but their top ten values. Then bring the groups together and list the values on a whiteboard, overhead projector, bulletin board, corkboard (using a storyboard approach), or some other means. Eliminate those values that are essentially the same though worded differently. Then ask the group to interact and narrow the remaining ones to no more than ten. It's okay to have eleven or twelve if they can't agree on ten.

Using a storyboard approach works with most groups. Once you have taught what values are and have shown several credos, ask the team to identify what they think their ministry's values are. This process involves one or two recorders who write the values on three-by-five-inch Post-it notes, using a black marker. Next, place the Post-its on a white or blackboard or the wall or some other appropriate place where all can see them. Once all the values are up, give each participant six red coding labels. Have them place these on what they believe are the six most important values. The six values that get the most red labels are the ministry's core values.

There are three advantages to discovering common values together. First, it's a bottom-up process as well as a top-down process. People at the grassroots level have a say as well as do the leaders at the top. Second, with everyone taking part in the process, all will get their fingerprints on the credo. This results in a ministry-wide ownership in the final product. Each person senses that he or she played a major part in determining the credo—these values are *my* values! Finally, because they have ownership and a sense of common cause, the chances are better that the people will live and minister by the values.

Comparing and Interpreting the Audit Results

Once you've completed the values-discovery process, the question becomes *What do you do with the results?* First, the individual and the organization will know its values and be able to develop a credo statement (the topic of the next chapter). That is understood going into the process. The ministry, however, can use the results when looking for a new leader, staff member, or volunteer, to search for common cause and build their leadership teams. To do so, use comparison and interpretation. Once you have discovered the values of the potential team members, compare them to the values of the ministry to determine if a ministry match exists. The ideal is to share all the same values. Since this isn't likely, even in a church or parachurch ministry, you'll need to look for common cause.

Pastor Andy and the board of Lake Country Church could have used the audits to discover their personal and corporate credos. The next step would have been to compare the two and interpret the results, determining common cause. If both potential pastor and board had ten core values, then common cause asks, *How many values do they share?* In the process of comparing their values, they might have discovered that they shared only three. This means that they agree on 30 percent of what is at the core. The bar graph in figure 2.2 represents this agreement.

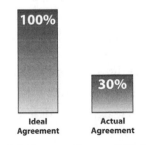

Figure 2.2. Common Cause—30% Agreement

What does this percentage of agreement mean for the ministry? How will it affect the working and leading relationships of the pastor and board? The general interpretation is that over several years of ministry they will likely agree on 30 percent of their decisions and disagree on 70 percent. The particular key values at issue would, of course, temper this. It's possible that a number of ministry decisions involve mostly the 30 percent where consensus exists. This means that they would agree much of the time—but don't count on it. The chances are even better that those ministry decisions would involve the 70 percent where they disagree. Thus, they would be at odds on practically everything of import.

The process could also be reversed. The pastor and the board might agree on 70 percent of their values and differ on only 30 percent as depicted in figure 2.3. The chances of a successful relationship have increased significantly. What is the best ratio for actual agreement? The answer depends on the board and the leader. Some can tolerate more disagreement than others. Some leaders have a proven track record as change agents. In general, I believe that agreement on seven to eight or more beliefs is necessary for a good partnership.

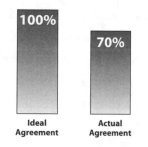

Figure 2.3. Common Cause—70% Agreement

One factor that influences the quality of the partnership is whether the ministry is growing, has leveled off, or is dying. Sometimes a dying ministry is willing to make changes that a growing or leveled off one isn't. Another influencing factor is the values themselves. Some are of such importance that they alone will affect common cause. One such value is the ministry's position on the Scriptures. Does the Bible direct all that we do, or does something else? A second value is creativity versus tradition. Does this church value the traditions of its past, or is it ready for change and the creation of new traditions?

HOW TO RESOLVE VALUES DIFFERENCES

This chapter is all about how to discover personal and corporate organizational values. The goal is that both the leaders and ministry organizations know their core values and articulate the same in a credo. But what happens when all have accomplished this and discover moderate to significant differences? If Pastor Andy and his board complete the values-discovery process and create a credo, they will find themselves in strong disagreement. What should they do?

One solution is to ignore these differences. Leaders do so to their peril, however. The differences are like dry tinder, waiting for a lightning spark or a carelessly discarded match to ignite them. The North American church terrain is strewn with the empty shells of charred ministries that belong to those who chose to ignore their values differences.

The answer and best solution is to pursue the value-resolution process. This was the response of the leadership of the early church in Acts 6:1–7 when the Grecian Jews complained that the Hebraic Jews were overlooking their widows in the distribution of food. The Twelve chose not to ignore the problem and God honored their efforts.

What is involved in the values-resolution process? I suggest the following six steps. First, bathe the entire process and all the people involved in prayer. James says, "You do not have, because you do not ask God" (James 4:2). Pray specifically about your differences. James also says, "The prayer of a righteous man is powerful and effective" (James 5:16). Ask those involved in the resolution process to pray together. Allow God to do his work with his people.

Second, study the Scriptures together. Hebrews 4:12 says that God's Word can penetrate the hearts of people as well as penetrate to the heart of an issue. As you study together, ask the basic nuts and bolts questions: Why are we here? Why do we do what we do? What are we doing? What are we supposed to be doing? How do we accomplish the ministry? Scripture answers these questions and more and, in the process, addresses the issues of the heart, personality differences, and most importantly, disparate values.

Third, be bold enough to acknowledge your differences and discuss them together. Conflict isn't new to the church—it has been a constant since the early church (Acts 5:1–10; 6:1–7; 15:1–21, 36–41). The early church's procedure was not to ignore or cover up their problems. Instead, they acknowledged them openly, discussed them together, and reached a resolution. We must take time to discuss our differences with one another and carefully listen to one another with a view toward resolution.

Fourth, pursue consensus not compromise. Most often people resolve their differences by compromising their positions. The idea is that everyone gives a little so that we can solve our problems and all can go home happy. Reality is that compromise rarely satisfies anyone and resolves few problems. Instead, people should agree to disagree. Then they must state what they believe and defend their positions. This is what took place at the Jerusalem Council in Acts 15. Normally, those who get the most votes win, but consensus says that the others agree to go along with them. If this isn't possible, then they're free to move on as Paul and Barnabas chose to do as described in Acts 15:36–41. The only restriction is that they not demean others in the process.

Fifth, it may be wise to work with an intermediary or consultant. This would likely involve spending money, but the results could be worth every penny and more. Some believe that the leader or pastor should function in this role. My experience is that few pastors are trained in or understand conflict resolution—most function as "prophets without honor" in their churches. The presence of an intermediary or consultant would disarm personal attacks, jettison much personal baggage, and keep the discussions focused on the issues. If the outside person is not able to help, this would be a sign that the ministry is in serious trouble and either needs a new board or a new leader.

Sixth, whatever the situation, there's a point where leaders must lead. The adage that you can't keep all the people happy all the time is true. Some pastors want to be liked and often fall into the trap of attempting to keep everyone in the church happy. Most lay boards are notorious for this—some view it as their primary function. The result is anemic leadership and unhappy congregants. In particular, those who know how to manipulate these pastors and boards will make a point of always being unhappy as a way to pursue their agendas for the ministry. Leaders must pursue the truth in love. This often means doing what is right and suffering the consequences. That's the price for being a leader. If the ministry can't live with that, then it's time for the leader to look for a new ministry. If the leader can't live with that, then he or she might not be a leader.

QUESTIONS FOR REFLECTION, DISCUSSION, AND APPLICATION

1. Are you convinced that you need to discover your core values or those of the ministry you work with? Why or why not?

2. Are you currently going through a values-formation period? If so, what are the circumstances? If you aren't, can you recall such a time in the past? What effect might such a time have on you or your ministry?

3. Who in your ministry is responsible for discovering the core organizational values? Did you include the point person? Did you include the key decision makers? Where are you in the process?

4. What are the core values of the point person? Any bad ones? What

are they? What are the core values of the organization that he or she serves? Any bad ones? What are they? Does the board agree among themselves on the ministry's essential values? Why or why not?

5. Do the leader of the ministry and the board differ on any values? If so, what are they? If you are the leader, how much actual agreement is necessary for you to take a ministry or remain in a ministry?

6. If you're the leader and you don't agree with your board on the ministry's essential values, what do you plan to do about it? If you're part of a board and you as a group don't agree with one another, what will you do about it? What if you don't agree as a board with the leader, what will you do about it?

3

The Development of Core Values

How to Construct Your Credo

ow should a church develop a statement of core values? What's involved in drafting a credo for a ministry? The answer is threefold. There exists a preparation phase, a process phase, and a determination phase.

THE PREPARATION FOR DRAFTING YOUR CREDO

Constructing a building has some things in common with constructing a values statement. One commonality is that both require some preparation before the process begins. The preparation for credo construction is deciding who develops the credo, the values that make up its credo, and the reasons why they should write the values down.

The Contractor of the Credo

Who is responsible for the construction of a ministry's credo? Just as the leadership is responsible to discover the values (see chapter 2), so it's responsible to develop the credo. When it's time to get something done, most look to their leaders for direction. In the church, the leaders are the pastoral team and the board. Both Pastor Andy and his board should see that the church develops a values statement that is tailor-made for itself. In the parachurch ministry, it's the point leader, such as the president or director, and the board who are responsible.

Shaping a ministry's core values, however, is preeminently the responsibility of the point person for the organization. The values that characterize most established organizations have also characterized their leaders. This has proved true in the marketplace with such individuals as Ross Perot formerly of EDS, Bill Gates of Microsoft, and Sam Walton of Wal-Mart. It is also true of Christian organizations formerly led by individuals such as James Dobson with Focus on the Family, Bill Bright with Campus Crusade, and Lorne Sanny of the Navigators.

Whether an entrepreneurial venture, such as those above, or a church, the core values are those of the point person. Then he or she invites others with similar beliefs to join the venture. In an established entity, the point person must consider the views of the board and the people before he or she joins them. The primary leader brings key values to the ministry, and the ministry already owns a set of critical values. This can be problematic, and if there exist substantial differences, I suggest that the potential leader not join the ministry. The other option is to attempt to change the ministry significantly or attempt to change one's own values. Either option, while possible, isn't promising.

The wise leader of an established ministry invites those in the ministry to join him or her in the values-development process. The size of a larger ministry such as a church of three hundred or more will limit lay involvement. The smaller ministry can expect more participation (see fig. 2.1). One option is to develop an initial ministry credo, then present it to a limited number of key lay leaders, giving them permission to change, add to, or approve it. I suggest that you use someone with language skills and creativity, such as a writer or teacher, to go over the document. Ask that person to review and fine-tune the product, but you don't want them to tamper with the actual values. Instead, they are to work only with the wording. They may need to word or reword the document in relevant, contemporary language that will communicate to those in the third millennium. The credos in appendix B provide examples that have gone through this process.

The Contractor's Building Blocks

Contractors don't create out of nothing—that is God's privilege alone. Contractors have to work with existing material; so do constructors of credos. The building blocks of the construction industry are wood, metal, cement, and so on. The building blocks of the ministry are the core organizational values. In particular, these values are the ones revealed in the values-discovery phase. At this point, most organizational values are like the house that the contractor has erected but has not finished. The walls are up and the roof is in place, but the structure is in need of paint and all the trim work.

You must remember throughout the process that you are working with the actual, not the aspirational, values. Again, an astute ministry constituency may view a ministry credo that consists primarily of aspirational values as hypocritical. But what does the established church that wants to be evangelistic but isn't there yet do with these aspirations? Can they put evangelism in their credo?

Aspirational values can be put in the credo if they are somehow marked as such. For example, you could place an asterisk beside them and note somewhere within the document what the asterisk represents. Another solution is to place the actual values together in one list and the desired (aspirational) values together in another. For the former, you could say that you are committed to the following values. For the latter, you might say that you aspire to, or are becoming an organization that implements, these values.

The Contractor's Blueprints

A contractor must have a written plan. It's called a blueprint. If he or she doesn't write down the plans, the result won't be a building or a house—it will be chaos. Credo contractors also must have a written plan. Written values clarify precisely what you believe. Writing forces you to think and be specific. If you know what your values are, you should be able to put them on a piece of paper. If you can't do that, then you need to do some more work in the values-identification and values-clarification phases.

Written values place the authority of the leadership behind the credo. Core values are a statement by the leadership of what the ministry values. Communicating them orally leaves room for noncompliance; communicating them in writing makes them official. When the leadership of the ministry pens the organization's values in ink, no one can plead ignorance should they violate those values. Thus, the leadership can enforce compliance from those who choose to ignore the values or who operate with a different set of values.

Numerous ways exist to communicate values—the life and example of the leadership, a message or sermon, storytelling, visual images, the ministry's language and metaphors, a brochure, what the ministry celebrates, and who its heroes are. A written statement, however, is a vital first step in the values-casting process. By writing, you put flesh on what may otherwise be sparse, abstract ideas, thus allowing them to spring to life in a fresh way that adds meaning and has impact on people's lives. In addition, a written credo will save you countless hours of explanation. People can first read what you value, then ask questions for clarification.

THE PROCESS OF DRAFTING YOUR CREDO

Once the foundation is laid, you are ready to construct your values statement. The process consists of three steps: determining the number of values, the actual values, and the values format.

Determine the Number of Values

The first step is to determine the number of values that will make up the credo. Answer the question, *How many beliefs should I have in my statement?* Since the average leader will have from fifty to as many as one hundred core values, how many should he or she include in a personal credo or that of the ministry organization?

A survey of the various credos for churches, parachurch ministries, and marketplace organizations reveals that values range in number from one to seventeen. In general, the marketplace organizations have the fewest. This is because they have been wrestling with these issues and asking these questions much longer than most churches. Hewlett-Packard is a business with only one driving value: "The HP way says, 'Do unto others as you would have them do unto you.' That's really what it's all about."[1] Ken Blanchard, a Christian and president of Blanchard Training and Development, has three core values: doing things right, building mutually satisfying partnerships, and accomplishing the company goals.[2] Two ministry organizations had the most values: CAM International, an independent missions organization, has fifteen; Saddleback Valley Community Church, a Southern Baptist church located in Orange County, California, has seventeen. The rest hovered somewhere between five and ten core values. In *Built to Last*, Collins and Porras note that visionary companies have from three to six.[3]

An important question is, *What is core?* The Jerusalem church included at least six values. Anything less than that would seem to leave out certain biblical essentials. With the exception of some churches, more than ten might indicate that they are not down to their core values, and may only serve to confuse people and frustrate the church's efforts.

The final verdict as to the number of core values lies with both the leadership and the individuals who make up the organization, and should be decided by consensus and not compromise. The final verdict rests with the leadership—those who are responsible to see that the ministry accomplishes its mission—and the constituency—those who are responsible to carry out that mission. The leadership and the missionaries of CAM International opted for fifteen. Any number less than fifteen left out what they believed were essentials.

As a consultant in this area for many years, I have come to believe that less is more. Thus, I limit the organizations (mostly churches) that I work with to six actual values. This limitation compels the organizations to focus on or really "get at" the core.

Once you have settled on the number of values, you may wish to arrange them in your credo in order of priority. Doing so says something about the most important of the important. That is why many organizations begin with a statement about the Scriptures and their commitment to them. The Bible is foundational to all the values that make up the credo.

In some situations, you might list them out of priority. You might feel that helping your people remember the values is more important than arranging them in order of importance. Consequently, you might form the credo around an acrostic. This involves taking the first letter of each value to form a memorable word such as the name of the ministry. For example, you will find the credo of Lakeview Community Church in appendix B. If it had eight values rather than seven, they could attempt to fashion each around the word *Lakeview*. The *L* could stand for lay ministry, the *A* for an active prayer ministry, and so on (see fig. 3.1). While an acrostic would help people remember the church's credo, it could also seem contrived. The ministry leadership, with the advice of the ministry constituency, will need to decide the issue.

L ay Ministry

A ctive Prayer

K ingdom Growth

E xposition of the Scriptures

V ital Community

I nnovation and Creativity

E xcellence

W orship

Figure 3.1. Sample Acrostic Credo

Determine the Actual Values

The second step in the process of developing the credo is to determine whether the beliefs on your list are values or something else. The reason for this step is that some values are often confused with the form that a value may take. An example is found in the credo of Lakeview Community Church of Cedar Hill, Texas (see appendix B). They have listed small groups as their fourth value:

A Commitment to Small Groups

We are committed to small-group ministry as one of the most effective means of building relationships, stimulating spiritual growth, and developing leaders.

The problem is that a small group is a form that a value takes and not the value itself. Every value has at least one form that implements it. A small group is the form that implements a value, such as authentic biblical community. Other values are evangelism, worship, prayer, teaching, and so on. All of these can take place in the context of a small group. Other values take other forms (see chart 3.1).

Value	Form
Authentic community	small group
Evangelism	crusade
Fellowship	potluck meal
Scripture	exposition

Chart 3.1. Forms of Values

The question is: How do you separate the two? How do you know which is the value and which is the form? There are two ways.

The first is to ask, *Is this an end or a means to an end?* The value is the end; the form is the means to an end. While values do have a greater end (to glorify God), in a sense they are an end in themselves. This is true of the values in chart 3.1 above. The forms that they take are a means to accomplish them. Therefore, if we ask, *Is our small-groups program an end in itself?* the answer is no. The groups are a means to an end such as an authentic biblical community. The same is true for conducting citywide crusades. Here we would ask, *Are we conducting these crusades as an end in themselves, simply to be putting on crusades? Or, are they the means to a greater end—evangelism?*

The second way to differentiate value from form is to ask, *Why are we doing what we are doing?* What you or your ministry are doing isn't the value. The reason you're doing it is the value. The *what* question brings to the surface the forms that serve to realize your values. The *why* question identifies your central values. Your church may be sponsoring a potluck meal once a month after church. That's the *what* or the *form*. The reason for the potluck meal is for fellowship.

Why is it so important to distinguish between the values and their forms? One reason is that the values, on the one hand, are timeless and should never change. The values that were important to the church in the first century are just as important to the church in the twenty-first century. They have not changed at all. Therefore, evangelism or worship is just as important today as in biblical times. On the other hand, the forms that the values take are timely. Scripture doesn't appear to hold any forms as sacrosanct. They can and should change from culture to culture and time to time because this is how the church or any other ministry remains relevant to the culture that it's trying to reach.

If leaders and their ministries wish to stay current and relate relevantly to the culture in which they desire to have an impact, they must regularly evaluate the forms and the programs that the values are expressed in to see if they are still having an impact. Value forms can grow stale and lose their ministry punch. When this happens, the ministry must change them or risk not having an effective ministry. Often the ministry will include the forms along with their values in the credo. This means that the credo will undergo some change when the ministry changes or adds a new form or method.

Determine the Values Format

A values format is the form that the values take when expressed in the credo. It includes the precise words, phrases, clauses, sentence structure, and other elements that communicate the organization's beliefs. There is no one correct values format that fits every church or parachurch ministry. Each ministry has to determine and develop one that best fits its culture and serves its people well. A review of the credos in appendix B and the Acadiana Community Church credo in appendix A demonstrates the different formats that various ministries use to express their beliefs. These may prove to be most helpful as you consider developing your own credo. As we look at some of them, you might find a format that fits your ministry context well.

That being said, my experience with churches is that most congregations desire a simple, straightforward format. Again, less is more! Therefore, I ask the churches I work with to format their values in the following way. First, they simply state what the value is. Second, they provide a brief definition or statement about the value or why it's even listed. This might include a Scripture verse or two. Finally, they include what I refer to as a "so-what statement" that is most often introduced by the term *therefore*. It explains how the value works itself out or is applied at the church. It's the value's application.

The closest example is that of Lakeview Community Church located in Cedar Hill, Texas, a suburb southeast of Dallas, Texas. The first value reflects the role that Scripture plays in their church:

A Commitment to Relevant Bible Exposition
We believe that the Bible is God's inspired Word, the authoritative and trustworthy rule of faith and practice for Christians. Therefore,

we are committed to equipping Christians, through the preaching
and teaching of God's Word, to follow Christ in every sphere of life.

They lead with a caption that includes the word *commitment*. It's followed
with an explanation of the value and an application. The latter is signaled
in several instances by the word *therefore*. I feel that the first sentence is
enough and the second isn't really needed.

QUESTIONS FOR REFLECTION, DISCUSSION, AND APPLICATION

1. Who in your ministry is responsible for crafting the credo? Is it the
   point person or primary leader? Are others involved in the process?
2. Are your values aspirational or actual? What is the difference? Will
   you include both in your credo? If yes, how will you do this to avoid
   confusing the two?
3. In constructing your credo, have you written your beliefs down? Why
   or why not? What are some reasons for writing them down?
4. How many values have you included in your credo? Why this number?
   Are they core? If you have more than ten, are there any you could
   drop? Are they listed in order of priority? Is this helpful or not? Would
   it help in communicating your core values to list them in an acrostic?
5. Have you checked your credo for any so-called values that are actually
   forms? What is the difference? Did you find any? What did you do
   about them?
6. Did you find any of the credos in appendixes A or B helpful in crafting
   your values credo? If yes, which ones?
7. Did you take the author's advice and format your credo similar to that
   of Lakeview Community Church?

Part 2

The Mission of Your Ministry

4

The Definition of Mission

What Is a Mission?

Developing a mission for your ministry is important for several reasons. First, the church needs a clear, compelling ministry direction. A well-focused mission statement provides the destination on the map toward which the entire ministry takes flight. It can then focus all its energy in a single direction. Second, the church desperately needs to know what it's supposed to be doing. A mission statement helps the ministry to determine precisely its biblical function. It answers the question, *What is the primary thing that God has called us to accomplish in this community?* Third, the church needs to look to the future. The mission statement predetermines the ministry's future. We cannot predict the future; however, the formulation of a succinct mission statement will help to create a ministry's preferred future. The development of a ministry mission also provides boundaries for decision making, inspires ministry unity, encourages helpful change, and shapes the ministry's strategies.

A most important question for pastors and their churches is definitional and developmental: What is a mission and how do you develop one for your church? The next chapter will address mission development. This chapter will define mission by discussing briefly what it isn't and then what it is. It will close with an examination of the various kinds of missions.

WHAT A MISSION IS NOT

People confuse a number of concepts with mission. In this section, I focus on the two most common misconceptions for mission—vision and purpose.

A Mission Isn't a Vision

The concept of mission is older than that of vision. A brief survey of books on the shelves of most libraries reveals that the word *mission* has been in use in management circles for a number of years. When I wrote *Developing a Vision for Ministry in the Twenty-first Century*, few, if any, were using the word *vision*. I was aware of only one other book on the topic by Southern Baptist pastor Robert Dale that proved to be far ahead of its time. There are few books totally devoted to vision even today. Many, however, refer to the concept in speech and in books relating to leadership and management.

As I travel and conduct seminars on leadership, I have come to expect the question, *What is the difference between a vision and a mission?* The words aren't synonyms as some leaders might think them to be. They have some elements in common but others that are different. This is such an important question that, rather than discuss it only briefly here, I have written chapter 7 to answer it. In chapter 7 I show that while the two concepts have at least four common characteristics, they differ from one another in at least eleven ways. They are, for example, defined differently, applied differently, are different in length, purpose, and activity.

A Mission Isn't a Purpose

My studies reveal that most people equate mission and purpose. They argue that an organization's purpose is to accomplish its mission. I believe that mission and purpose are different for Christian organizations in at least three ways. First, the mission asks the *what* question: What has God called this ministry to accomplish? The answer to this question is the organization's mission. The purpose, however, asks and answers an entirely different question. It answers the *why* question: Why has God placed you here? The answer is the organization's purpose. It is the reason why the ministry does what it does (its mission).

There is a second distinction—the mission serves as a target at which the ministry takes aim. In the case of the church, that target is the Great Commission (Matt. 28:19–20; Mark 16:15). The church's mission is to make disciples. The ministry organization's purpose, however, goes far beyond its target—it is the organization's reason for being. It is much more fundamental to the ministry. Whereas the church's mission is the Great Commission, its purpose is to glorify God (Pss. 22:23; 50:15; Isa. 24:15; Rom. 15:6; 1 Cor. 6:20; 10:31). The mission *serves* the purpose, but the mission is not the same as the purpose.

The third distinction further clarifies the second. Not only does the mission come under the umbrella of the purpose of the organization but so do a number of other ministry concepts. A ministry's core values—the topic of chapters 1 through 3—exist to glorify God. The same is true of the vision, strategy, and other vital ministry elements. Like the ministry mission, they too serve the purpose but are not the same as the purpose.

WHAT A MISSION IS

Often it helps to discover what something is by examining first what it isn't. Now that we have done this and have eliminated two confusing elements, it's time for a definition. I define a ministry mission as *a broad, brief, biblical statement of what the organization is supposed to be doing.* This definition contains five essential elements.

A Mission Is Broad

The first defining element is breadth. It is essential that a ministry's mission be broad or all-embracing. The institution's master goal takes precedence over all its other goals. Mission is the umbrella over all the institution's ministry activities. This means that all the goals and activities should fit comfortably under the overarching ministry mission. If a goal or activity doesn't fit under the mission, then either the mission isn't broad enough or the goal or activity isn't within the scope of the mission and should be discontinued.

The following is the mission statement of Matthew Road Baptist Church located in Grand Prairie, Texas.

> Our mission is to share the love of God with the people of the mid-cities and beyond so that they can become fully devoted followers of Christ.

This mission is broad and includes all that Christ has commissioned the church to do. Essentially, the Great Commission divides into evangelism and edification. Everything a church can do would fit under one or the other. We find evangelism and edification in Matthew Road Baptist's mission statement. The church begins with sharing the love of God. That is evangelism. Its mission doesn't stop there, however. It moves new believers and established Christians toward maturity, toward being "fully devoted followers of Christ."

While a mission needs breadth, it should not be too broad. Too much breadth serves only to confuse followers and says very little. The following is a fictitious mission statement for an inner-city ministry.

> The mission of the Metroplex Foundation is to provide a "city of hope" for all its citizens where God is glorified.

This is too broad. It doesn't say anything. For example, what is a "city of hope"? I would assume that because it's a mission to the inner city it is trying to bring hope to people living in the inner city. But what does that mean? Is it hope as found in Christ? Is it leading people to faith in Christ, or does it involve only feeding people? This ministry statement is too vague to have any impact. In addition, the problem is compounded by including the phrase "where God is glorified." What does that mean? I suspect that it means different things to different people. The important question is, *What does it mean to the ministry organization?* It isn't wrong to include a statement about glorifying Christ or God—that is very biblical. It would be much clearer, however, to replace it with a brief statement that says specifically how God is being glorified.

A Mission Is Brief

The second defining element of a mission statement is brevity. Brevity determines the size or length of a mission statement. No standard or fixed regulation exists for the size or length of a mission statement, and a cursory examination of corporate mission statements reveals a variety. I argue that the mission statement should be short. Some say that it should be limited to fifteen or twenty pages in length. Others say that it should be one page or less. My response is that both are too long. Fifteen to twenty pages is excessive, and even one page is too much.

How short is brief? I believe that a good mission statement can and should be no more than a single sentence. My experience has been that the best mission statements are single, well-written sentences. A characteristic of highly effective organizations, no matter how complex, is that they can summarize what they're supposed to be doing in a succinct, simple way.

Randy Frazee, the senior pastor of Pantego Bible Church in Arlington, Texas, tells the following story of a meeting that his church administrator attended where Peter Drucker was the main speaker. A participant asked Drucker how long a mission statement should be. He responded, "If you can get the mission statement on a T-shirt, then it's probably the appropriate length."[1] Therefore, the critical test for a mission statement is whether it passes the T-shirt test; is it short enough to fit on a T-shirt?

Several churches have developed excellent mission statements that illustrate the value of a single-sentence mission statement. Willow Creek Community Church, located in Barrington, Illinois, developed this succinct statement:

> Our mission is to turn irreligious people into fully devoted followers of Christ.

In this case, Willow Creek could have used several pages to explain what the phrase *fully devoted follower of Christ* is. No doubt some people would appreciate and gain from this knowledge; however, such length would have served only to bury most of their people in minutiae.

There are several reasons why good mission statements are brief. The first is communication. A key to clear, effective communication is brevity, not verbosity. People tend to read and pay more attention to short written statements, not to those of one or more pages. Second, short statements are more easily understood. More information may not clarify but only serve to confuse. Third, people remember succinct sentences. Once you add a second sentence or a third, congregants will abandon any attempt to memorize the mission.

A Mission Is Biblical

People have used the word *biblical* in a number of ways. One is that if a mission is biblical, it has to be found in the Bible. This means that every church and parachurch ministry must find their mission somewhere within Scripture. Those who develop the mission statement are to search through the Bible until they find a verse that gives them a mission. Then, that verse essentially becomes the mission. This view is quite restrictive. I prefer the view that a biblical mission agrees with Scripture. While it doesn't necessarily have to be found in the pages of the Bible, it must not disagree with the teaching of Scripture.

A biblical mission is from God. He is the source of all missions. He may reveal your mission through the Bible or he may use some other means. Again, the mission must agree with, not contradict, the Bible. There are numerous mission statements that are sprinkled throughout the Old and New Testaments that are clearly from God. Let's briefly examine five in the Old Testament. The first belongs to Adam and Eve. God communicates their mission statement in Genesis 1:28: "God blessed them and said to them, 'Be fruitful and increase in number; fill the earth and subdue it. Rule over the fish of the sea and the birds of the air and over every living creature that moves on the ground.'" They were to have dominion over creation.

A second is Moses' mission. God revealed it to Moses in Exodus 3:10: "So now, go. I am sending you to Pharaoh to bring my people the Israelites out of Egypt." This one sentence sums up this leader's mission that extended over all that took place as recorded in Genesis through Deuteronomy.

A third is Joshua's mission. God presents it in Joshua 1:2: "Moses my servant is dead. Now then, you and all these people, get ready to cross the Jordan River into the land I am about to give them—to the Israelites." God's mission was to move Israel out of Egypt and into Canaan. He used two leaders with separate missions to accomplish his mission. Moses was to lead God's people out of bondage in Egypt. Joshua was to lead them into Canaan—the Promised Land.

A fourth is Isaiah's mission. In Isaiah 6:9–10 God commands the prophet, "Go and tell this people: 'Be ever hearing, but never understanding; be ever seeing, but never perceiving. Make the heart of this people callused; make their ears dull and close their eyes. Otherwise they might see with their eyes, hear with their ears, understand with their hearts, and turn and be healed.'" This must have been a frustrating mission for Isaiah. It was to result in little spiritual progress.

A fifth is Jeremiah's mission statement. The Lord communicates it in Jeremiah 1:10: "See, today I appoint you over nations and kingdoms to uproot and tear down, to destroy and overthrow, to build and to plant."

In short, Jeremiah's mission was to proclaim to God's people a message of blessing and judgment.

There are several mission statements in the New Testament. One is the Savior's. His God-given mission is revealed in Mark 10:45: "For even the Son of Man did not come to be served, but to serve, and to give his life as a ransom for many." Jesus' mission was one of service. He would serve humankind to the point that he would pay the ultimate price—the sacrifice of his life for the sins of the world.

God has also given the church its mission. Matthew recorded it in Matthew 28:19: "Therefore go and make disciples of all nations." Mark recorded the same in Mark 16:15: "Go into all the world and preach the good news to all creation." It's the Great Commission mission that involves moving people from wherever they are in their relationship to God (lost or saved) to where God wants them to be (mature). The reason that the early church's mission is so important to us in the present is that its mission is our mission. The mission that Christ gave to the church in the first century is the same that he gives to us for the twenty-first century. I've provided chart 4.1 so you can see all the Great Commission passages together and the distinctives of each.

Scripture	Who	What	To Whom	How	Where
Matt. 28:19–20	11 Disciples	Go, make disciples	All nations	Baptizing and teaching	—
Mark 16:15	11 Disciples	Go, preach the good news	All creation	—	All the world
Luke 24:46–48	11 Disciples	Be witnesses	All nations	Preaching repentance and forgiveness of sins	Beginning from Jerusalem
Acts 1:8	11 Disciples	Be witnesses	—	With power	Jerusalem, Judea, and Samaria and the uttermost parts of the world

Chart 4.1. The Great Commission

A Mission Is a Statement

A fourth defining element is that the mission is a statement. Every ministry must articulate its mission in some type of statement if its people are to know and understand their overall goal. This is a major problem for many churches across North America. Most haven't articulated a mission statement. Most likely, this is because they don't have one.

A mission statement may be verbal or written; however, I believe that leaders best communicate their *visions* with verbal statements and their *missions* with written statements. When people see the mission statement on paper, they know in their heads where the ministry is going. Writing out the mission in the form of a statement forces you to gather your thoughts and clearly think through what you're saying. When a leader can clearly write his or her mission on paper, then most likely it is a well-thought-through statement.

Writing out the mission statement puts it in a form that you can communicate in a variety of ways. One is to place it prominently on the church's bulletin, brochure, or newsletter where all can see it and be regularly reminded of it. Another is to include it in a statement that is read and discussed in classes for newcomers or new members, an inclusion that is imperative because new members and interested people must obtain ownership of the mission in order to be involved with the ministry. The mission could be framed or put on a wall plaque and hung in a church's foyer or its main offices. You could place it on wallet-sized cards for the people who are a part of the ministry to keep with them, or follow Peter Drucker's advice and actually put it on a T-shirt. Then people could wear it around the house as well as around the ministry. It would serve as a constant reminder of the ministry's mission.

A Mission Is What God Wants the Ministry to Accomplish

A fifth defining element is that a mission is what the ministry is supposed to accomplish. It's your ministry's primary goal or task. It's what "business" you're in. It's not what you want to do, but what God wants you to do. The vital mission question is, *What does God want your church to accomplish?* This appears to be such a simple question, yet too few ministry organizations are asking it. A major reason for the decline of so many churches that were vibrant in the 1940s and 1950s is that they have forgotten their mission or what business they are in. Most if not all began with a leader who had a clear mission for the church. That mission had much to do with why the church was planted. With the passing of time and a relative degree of success, however, that mission has been lost and left behind while the institution moves forward.

A key to revitalizing many of these churches and similar ministries is to ask the mission question. Peter Drucker writes, "We are mission-focused. What are we trying to do? Don't ever forget that first question. The mission must come first. This is the lesson of the last fifty to one hundred years. The moment we lose sight of the mission we are gone."[2] The same is true for church planting. A new church must begin with a clear mission that is strategically positioned in such a way that no one forgets it with the passing of time.

The mission question, *What does God want our church to do?* is directional and diagnostic. It is *directional* for new ministries whether church or parachurch. When they answer this question, they know where they are supposed to be going and what they are supposed to be doing.

The mission question is *diagnostic* for older, established ministries. It is the first of seven questions below that comprise the ministry mission audit, which will help a ministry diagnose its state of existence.

Ministry Mission Audit

1. The answer to the first question, *What does God want us to do?* takes the ministry to the Bible. Do the Scriptures directly or indirectly answer this question? We saw above that the church's mission is the Great Commission: pursuing lost people, reaching lost people, and then discipling them (Matt. 20:19–20). So, the first diagnostic ques-

tion is, *Are we pursuing and winning lost people and then helping them mature in the faith?* People themselves are responsible to grow, but the church is responsible to put in place a strategy to help them grow.

2. The second diagnostic question is, *What are we doing?* While Christ has commissioned the church to make disciples, far too many aren't accomplishing this task today. Some function much as a convalescent home. They have people who are saying, "Look, I've done my part, now it's time for somebody else to take care of me." The problem is that there are fewer young people around to take care of them. Others function as safe cognitive communities. They are one big happy (and in some cases not-so-happy) Bible study group. They know much about the Bible, but not many people outside the community come to faith. Others are evangelistic centers where people come to faith in Christ but fall into nominal Christianity because there is no program to take them any further in Christlikeness.

3. The third diagnostic question assumes that there is a discrepancy between questions one and two. It asks, *Why aren't we doing what God want us to be doing?* When you ask this question in a church board meeting, people quickly become uncomfortable. They shift in their seats and clear their throats, and the room becomes strangely quiet. The most common answer is that today's typical church has become inward focused. They are simply trying to take care of their current congregations and to keep the doors open. Another answer is that the pastor is strong in an area such as preaching but not in evangelism. Other answers are disobedience, fatigue, hidden agendas, ignorance, and so on.

4. The fourth question forces people to look to the institution's future if it has no biblical mission. It asks, *If we continue on our present course, where will the ministry be two, five, or ten years from now?* The answer for a growing church is that it levels off. The answer for a leveled off church is that it declines. And the answer for a declining church is that it no longer exists.

5. The fifth question focuses on the leadership. It asks, *Do our key leaders know where the ministry is and where it's going?* It also asks, *Do they agree on that direction?* My experience with some older, traditional churches that are struggling is that they are ignoring the present and the future while looking to and wishing for a return to the past.

6. The sixth question assumes that the ministry is merely circling the airport or is flying off course. It asks, *What will it take to change course and move in a God-ordained direction?* The answer is critical. A good answer is, *Whatever it takes—as long as it doesn't contradict Scripture.* But this is difficult for ministries that have been pursuing other missions for years. Another answer is, *A miracle.* Most often, this is the answer of a dying ministry. There is not much hope here.

7. The final question is, *Are we, individually and corporately, willing to do whatever it takes to move the ministry in a new direction?* Essentially, this is an obedience issue. The call is for repentance and response to God's clear directive in his Word. It's much easier to talk about than to accomplish. Failure to act places the entire ministry in jeopardy, and long-term disobedience may result in the death of the institution, as happened to the churches in Revelation 2 and 3.

Ministry Mission Audit Summary

1. According to Scripture, what does God want you to do?
2. What are you doing?
3. If there's a discrepancy, why aren't you doing what God wants you to do?
4. If you continue on your present course, where will the ministry be two, five, or ten years from now?
5. Do your key leaders know where the ministry is and where it's going?
6. What will it take to change course and move in a God-ordained direction?
7. Are you and the leadership willing to do whatever it takes to move the ministry in a new direction?

KINDS OF MISSIONS

When we covered the ministry's core values earlier in this book, we discovered various kinds of values: conscious versus unconscious, shared versus unshared, and so forth. Most of those same categories hold true for the church's mission. Following are five:

A Conscious Versus an Unconscious Mission

Most churches have a mission whether or not they know it or can verbalize it. As I said in the previous chapter on values, your actual values will drive or take you somewhere. The ministry ship is moving toward some ministry port. That "somewhere" is the church's mission. The church, however, may not be aware of where its values are taking it. Thus, it needs to move that mission from an unconscious to a conscious level so that it can know what its mission is. It must discover and articulate its actual mission.

The way to accomplish this is to look at the church's values and determine where they are taking the church. When consulting with a church, I list its core values on a whiteboard, and ask the strategic leadership team the question, *Where have these values taken you?* The answer is the church's ministry mission. Next, I ask the team to articulate that mission in a written statement so that they can hold it and work with it at a conscious level.

A Personal Versus an Organizational Mission

While the church as a whole has a mission, most individuals, whether they know it or not, have a mission in mind for the church as well. The first is the organizational mission, and the second is a personal mission. I suspect that an individual's personal ministry mission is formed early in his or her life. This formation may have taken place in the church where that person came to faith—the individual embraced that church's mission as his or her own. Or it may have occurred later in a church or ministry that was vibrant for Christ. Regardless of the circumstances, it has marked each person for life, and that individual brings this mission with him or her to your church.

The same is true for the senior or only pastor of a church and his or her staff. Most pastors have personal ministry missions that they bring with them when churches hire them. Again, while some pastors are aware of their personal missions, most are not.

Consequently, I would argue that any church address the issue of personal mission. People must know that their pastor's personal mission may be different than their church's mission, and that the latter must prevail or the church will attempt to move in many directions at the same time. This means that the church will pull apart rather than join together.

The people of the church must work with a prospective senior pastor or staff member and attempt to discover what his or her personal mission is before inviting that person to pastor and minister to the church. And those of you who are pastors and staff must ask the same question of both yourself and the church to maximize the effects of your placement.

I'll say more about personal and organizational or congregational missions below.

A Shared Versus an Unshared Mission

Some churches have consciously developed and articulated a mission statement, but most have not. Regardless, once the church has articulated such a statement, it may discover that some or even many of its people do not share the same mission. People join churches for different reasons and, as stated above, many bring their own personal missions with them.

The problem is that a shared ministry mission is essential to the church's effectiveness, whereas unshared ministry missions lead to disunity and hold a potential for disaster. Again, they pull people apart. Therefore, it is important that a church address the issue of ministry mission with its congregants. A good time and place to do so is when a person joins the church. I'm convinced that every church should have a new members class where it orients new people to its values, mission, vision, and strategy as well as other matters such as doctrine. The idea is to get people on the "same page" at the beginning of their church experience to achieve maximum ministry effectiveness.

A Correct Versus an Incorrect Mission

While most or all churches have a ministry mission, it may not be the correct mission. My experience is that most churches fall into this latter category. More than two thousand years ago, the Savior predetermined and gave the church its biblical mission. It is the Great Commission—to make (evangelize) and mature (edify) believers (Matt. 28:19–20; Mark 16:15; and so forth). A church that pursues any other mission is pursuing the wrong mission no matter how noble that mission might be. A teaching church's mission, for example, would be to preach the Bible. A worship-oriented church's mission would be to worship God. Another church's mission, often but not always smaller churches, is fellowship. Do not misunderstand what I am saying. These are all good things that are found in the Bible, but they, by themselves, are not the Great Commission! They may lead to the Great Commission, but are not the totality of it.

Therefore, it is imperative that once a church discovers its mission, it asks itself the question, *Is our mission the correct mission? Is it the Great Commission?* If the answer is fuzzy or an outright no, the church will need to change its mission from whatever it is to what the Savior has determined that it be—the Great Commission. To continue to pursue the wrong or incorrect mission is disobedience and a violation of Scripture.

An Actual Versus an Aspirational Mission

As with its core values, a church may have an actual versus an aspirational mission. The actual mission is where its values are taking it as described above. However, if this is an incorrect mission, then it will need to embrace a Great Commission mission. The churches that I consult with discover this quickly and adopt a Great Commission mission.

It is imperative, though, that a church understand that the new, correct mission is only aspirational at this point in time. Many assume that the new mission is now their actual mission when in fact it is still aspirational. It will not become their actual mission until the church changes, and consequently owns the mission. And this takes time. How can the church accomplish this kind of change so that it embraces the new, correct, biblical mission? The answer is to return to its actual values. It may need to change some values or, better, embrace those that will lead it to the correct mission. A list of these values are found in Acts 2:41–47, and the key value in that list is evangelism. Evangelism serves as the "bookends," in fact, for the other values (see vv. 41–42). I would go so far as to argue that if a church does not hold evangelism as a core value, it cannot become a Great Commission church. Regardless, core values are the key to adopting in time the correct, biblical mission.

PERSONAL, ORGANIZATIONAL, AND DEPARTMENTAL MISSIONS

So far we have talked about organizational mission. That is because it's the topic of this book. Your organizational mission, however, is not the priority; your personal mission is.

Personal Mission

What your organizational mission is to your ministry, your personal mission is to your life. Therefore, the development of your personal mission should precede that of your organizational mission. Your personal mission determines what you will do with your life and how you'll serve Christ. This, in turn, may lead to your service in a particular ministry organization. Once you have determined this and have aligned with that organization, you are ready to develop a mission for that organization.

I encourage you to develop a personal mission statement before you develop your organizational mission statement. Here are some questions, and your answers will help you determine your mission in life:

1. What do you want to do with your life?
2. What does God want you to do with your life?
3. If God gave you one wish for your life, what would it be?
4. What legacy do you want to leave behind?
5. How do you want others—your friends and family—to remember you after you're gone?

If you are in your twenties or thirties, you may struggle with these questions. The reason is that you may not have had much experience in life or ministry, so you're unsure of your answers. Should this be your situation, I encourage you to pursue the discovery of your divine design. It consists of your natural and spiritual gifts, your talents and abilities, your passion (what you feel strongly about), your temperament, and many other things.

Writing a personal mission statement helps you to determine what God wants you to do with your life. That is most important. It also assists you in making good decisions about matters that affect your life. Say, for example, that an organization offers you a position. Now you have to make a decision: Do I go with them and move on, or do I stay where I am? You evaluate your options and make a decision based on your mission statement. Such decisions will serve to refine your mission statement because they will teach you much about yourself. A personal mission statement can make the difference between mediocre service for Christ and exceptional service. Writing for the marketplace, Michael Gerber says, "I believe it's true that the difference between great people and everyone else is that great people create their lives actively, while everyone else is created by their lives, passively waiting to see where life takes them next."[3] Gerber's words remind me of Paul's in 1 Corinthians 9:24, "Do you not know that in a race all the runners run, but only one gets the prize? Run in such a way as to get the prize."

Organizational Mission

Once you have determined your personal mission in life, then you are ready to develop an organizational or, for most, a congregational mission. I use the word *organizational*. Other words that also apply are *congregational*, *institutional*, and *corporate*. The organizational mission should be in line with your personal mission. For example, God may have designed you to lead a church as its pastor. Therefore, you as the pastor of the church should develop its organizational mission by implementing the Great Commission through the local church ministry.

Departmental Mission

The departmental mission is under the umbrella of the organization's mission. As a church or parachurch ministry grows in size, it will organize itself into different departments. A church might have departments responsible for worship, for example, or Christian education, evangelism, and so on. Each of these departments should develop its own mission statement to show how it contributes to the overall, or master, mission of the ministry.

The departmental mission has three benefits. First, it brings the mission concept down to the grassroots level. It emphasizes, and serves as a constant reminder of, the importance of mission and what the organization as well as the department is all about. Second, it shows how each department contributes to the whole, demonstrating the importance of each department in accomplishing the overall mission of the organization. It announces to all that everyone is an important part of the institution and that everyone has a vital stake in it. Finally, it serves to keep each department focused on what not only the institution is supposed to be doing but what each department is supposed to be doing. This discourages either from moving off in its own direction.

Not long ago I visited and toured Willow Creek Community Church. As I walked by the various departments within the church, I noticed that they had mounted each department's mission statement on a prominent wall in each area.

Dallas Seminary is a parachurch organization that has an institutional mission. Since it's one of the larger seminaries, it consists of a number of departments such as Christian education, languages, field education, human resources, and so on. One department is the physical plant that is responsible for maintaining the facilities that are vital to the school's operation. The physical plant has developed the following mission statement:

> The mission of the physical plant is to serve the Dallas Theological Seminary community with a professional and personable attitude by providing a physical environment that is conducive to the DTS mission of preparing godly servant-leaders in the body of Christ worldwide.

QUESTIONS FOR REFLECTION, DISCUSSION, AND APPLICATION

1. Do you have a personal mission statement? Are you convinced of the importance of such a statement? Why or why not? How might a personal mission statement make a difference in your life?

2. Does your ministry organization have a mission statement? If yes, what is it? Is it a good one? If the organization doesn't, then why not?

3. What is your ministry supposed to be doing? What is it actually doing? Are your answers to these two questions the same or is there a discrepancy between them? If there's a discrepancy, how do you explain it?

4. If your ministry continues on its present course, where do you envision it in two years? In five years? In ten years?

5. Does the primary leader of the ministry and the board know where the ministry is presently and where it's going? Why or why not?

6. What will it take for your ministry to change and do what it's supposed to do? Is the leadership (president, pastor, board) willing to change? Why or why not? Are the people willing to change? Explain.

5

The Development of a Mission

How to Make Your Mission

How do you develop a coherent, biblical mission statement? The answer is three *p* words: *personnel*, *preparation*, and *process*. I have designed this chapter to help you work your way through the three *ps* as you develop a mission statement for your ministry.

MISSION DEVELOPMENT PERSONNEL

It's imperative that farmers farm. If others such as those who finance the farmer or those who sell him his equipment should attempt to replace the farmer, the results would be disastrous. The first *p* stands for the ministry personnel who make up the mission-development team. The right people must be involved in the process. The questions are these: Who are the right people? Who should develop the mission statement?

I advise most church and parachurch ministries to try the following. The pastor or lead person initiates and develops a mission. This is an essential act of leadership that involves placing an initial document on the table. Then, other vital people who are on the leadership team are invited to review and evaluate it. My experience is that it's most difficult for a group of people to design a mission statement from nothing. Having a lead person prepare a draft gives the leadership team an idea of what you are attempting to do and something to react to as well. It allows them to get their fingerprints all over the statement and experience a sense of ownership.

The most effective mission statements reflect the hearts of their people. A mission has to be something that both the leadership and the people can share. Peter Drucker points out that it's your people who determine the performance capacity of your organization. More importantly, the New Testament teaches the same principle (Eph. 4; 1 Cor. 12; Rom. 12). If your people don't feel some ownership, then they aren't likely to commit to the mission. It then becomes your mission, not their mission.

How many people should you involve? The general principle is that too many cooks spoil the broth. In chapters 2 and 3 we learned that the size of the ministry directly affects those who are involved. If the ministry is a small church, it can include some of its members as well as its leaders (see fig. 2.1), which elicits more input from those at the grassroots level. You find out what is on the hearts of the men and women in the pews. The downside is that this method allows the church's squeaky wheels—those who resist change—to express their opinions.

A larger ministry will not be able to involve many people at the grassroots level due to its sheer size. These ministries will depend on the senior pastor, the staff, the board, other key leaders, and small-group leaders who represent the various segments of the congregation. These people are to give input and help develop the ministry mission. Some churches would be wise to conduct "town hall" meetings at which the senior pastor and staff present the mission and elicit responses from the congregation at large. You should keep in mind, however, that too much input from too many people will only serve to neuter a good mission statement. Finally, whether a large or small church, it is wise to have the congregation vote on the mission statement because it affects the direction of the entire church.

I also suggest that you consider the use of a consultant in developing your mission as well as your core values, vision, and other key concepts. It's important that you do the ministry nuts and bolts well. A qualified, skilled consultant brings much knowledge and expertise to the process, including fresh objectivity. He or she will save you time, and the quality of the product will more than offset expenses. As a consultant, I most often work with a larger group of people—what I refer to as a Strategic Leadership Team of twenty-five to thirty people. The advantage is that they develop the mission statement, and they come away from the process owning the mission statement and unified in its direction. Such shared commitment is rare in most churches. If you feel that you have the skills and abilities to work with such a large group, then I would recommend that you pursue this approach over those suggested above.

MISSION DEVELOPMENT PREPARATION

The temptation for many leaders is to move too quickly. They want to jump immediately into the mission-development process. However, preparation must precede process. The seasoned farmer knows that before he plants his crops he must prepare the soil, or an anemic harvest will be the result. The mission-development process also requires the preparation of the ministry soil if it is to produce a healthy fruitful mission statement. The preparation stage consists of answering five critical questions.

Is There a Need for a Ministry Mission?

The answer to this question at this point seems obvious and perhaps even silly. It may not be obvious or silly, however, to certain board members. They may not have read about these basic ministry concepts and are reeling in the wake of all the change that is crashing in around them as they move into the twenty-first century. Many have assumed a defensive posture, hoping that all the turbulence will blow over and that life will return to normal very soon.

The answer is not as obvious, either, to those who are currently in a successful ministry. Why develop a mission statement when everything is going well? As the old-timer once quipped, "If it ain't broke, why fix it?" My point is that if those responsible for developing a ministry mission don't see the need, then you're wasting your time. In some situations, you could cause your ministry harm by pursuing such a venture. People resist and even resent doing something for which they don't feel a sense of need.

Regardless of where people are regarding the need, you would be wise to take time to prepare the soil for the mission seed. The best way to accomplish this is to follow the lead of Pastor Andy and take the ministry mission audit presented in the previous chapter. The lead person in a parachurch ministry and the pastor of a church should take it first. Then they should lead their boards and relevant personnel through the process as well.

Is the Ministry Ready for a Mission?

If the ministry sees a need for developing a mission, then the ministry would seem to be ready for a mission. Even if the need is realized, however, a ministry may not be ready to proceed because of busyness, for example. A church leader may be so busy trying to keep the church afloat and still do the work of the ministry that he or she believes there is not enough time to develop a mission. It becomes just one more burdensome item on the ministry to-do list. What the leader doesn't realize is that a dynamic mission statement has the potential to mobilize some of the inactive people so that they become more involved in the ministry and thus take some of the load off him or her.

Another reason against proceeding is hopelessness. The ministry is dying and is at a point of no return. Those few stalwarts who have stayed with the ministry feel that to invest further effort in trying to keep the ministry alive is futile. It would be akin to investing in a business that is on its last leg. A dynamic mission statement, however, has the potential to breathe life-giving oxygen into a dying ministry and revive it.

How Much Time Will It Take to Develop a Mission?

There's a popular maxim: If anything is worth doing, then it's worth doing well. The question is, *How much time should you set aside if you want to develop an excellent mission statement?* While it will take some quality time if it's to be done well, it will not take as much time as some of the other ministry ABCs such as the core values, the vision, and the strategy.

It's conceivable that a team of leaders could develop a well-prepared mission statement in three to five sessions that last several hours each with some reflective time in between. Much depends on how well the team works together. My experience is that most team problems are either philosophical or relational, not theological. If there is initial agreement on the core values of the team members, as well as on vision and other key areas of culture, the development session will go much faster. When I conduct mission-development sessions with unified boards, we average from one to two hours, providing they agree on their core values. This is another reason why I advise ministries to develop their core values before their mission statements.

Preparation is important because the more that team members know about mission development going into the process, the better. A book like this one can prove helpful and save much time in preparing the soil. Also, it is difficult to create an original mission statement. You may want to provide the team with a number of sample mission statements that will prod their thinking. You might benefit by using some of those provided later in this chapter.

Where Is the Best Place to Develop a Mission?

Because developing a mission statement takes less time than some of the other basics, you may want to use your own facilities, such as the church building instead of going to a retreat setting. Using your own facilities affords several advantages. One is that you don't have to sleep in a strange place, which is problematic for some who find it difficult to sleep in a place that they aren't accustomed to. A second is that you don't have to spend any time away from your family. A third is that you have all the equipment you need with you. Invariably, when a team takes a planned retreat, they leave some important item behind. Finally, you don't waste any time traveling. Using your own facilities, though, has its disadvantages, such as interruptions and distractions. You aren't very far from the telephone or individuals who believe that their problems are major emergencies that must be dealt with immediately.

Some people prefer to get away from home. Often a different environment can better spark the creative processes than a familiar one. People like to retreat to a mountain home or a nearby lake. They find that this allows more time for intense, creative reflection. They are able to focus more on the problems and issues at hand when they are away. Also, they are better able to enjoy one another's company.

If you decide on a retreat setting, the distance traveled can be long or short. I went on a retreat with a board from a church in Dallas, Texas. We traveled to Branson, Missouri, where we held our meetings in a motel located on a mountain lake. One of the elders flew us there in his own plane, and we were gone for only a day. One of the departments at Dallas Seminary chose to retreat to a health facility only a block away that provides rooms for meetings. When the day was over, the team had the option to swim, sit in the sauna, jog, or use the workout equipment before going home. My home church opted to retreat to a western ranch about twenty miles out of town. The ranch had special facilities for group meetings, and at the end of the day the staff finished their time together with a sumptuous steak supper.

How Much Will It Cost to Develop a Mission?

Most professional people value their time more than their money. Thus, this question is important. Actually, your answer to the previous question affects your answer to this question. If you use your own facilities, the cost will be minimal. You might choose to take the team out for a hearty lunch or a steak supper. Some local institutions such as banks have meeting rooms that they allow others to use as a courtesy.

If you travel to some off-site location, the cost will be greater. You will need to budget for travel expenses such as gasoline and wear and tear on automobiles. You will also need to allow for the rental of several rooms, refreshments, and meals.

The bottom line is to answer the question, *How much is it worth to your ministry to have the best mission statement possible?* The answer is that it could make the difference between the success and failure of the ministry institution.

MISSION DEVELOPMENT PROCESS

Once you know who is going to develop the ministry mission (the mission personnel) and you have prepared the soil (the mission preparation), the third *p* is the mission process. What is that process? What are the steps that you and your team should take to develop the mission product? You'll find the answer in the definition of the mission. In chapter 4 I defined a ministry mission as "a broad, brief, biblical statement of what your organization is supposed to be doing." This definition is key to the mission development process. If you can remember the definition, you can also remember the process.

The way to develop your mission is to use each of the key elements in the definition as a step in the process. The rest of this chapter will examine these elements as we walk through the process. For your working convenience, I have included a summary of this process in appendix E.

Step 1: Determine What You're Supposed to Be Doing According to the Scriptures

The first step begins with the last element in the definition, that it is a statement of what your organization is supposed to be doing. It combines with the third that says it should be biblical. The direct or indirect source of your mission is the Bible. What does the Bible say that your church or para church ministry should be doing? Answering this question means that God determines your mission. Three miniquestions will aid you with step one.

1. *Are you involved in a church or parachurch ministry?* You may categorize a Christian ministry as either church or parachurch. If you serve Christ in a church, then he has already predetermined your ministry mission. It's the Great Commission as found in Matthew 28:19–20 and Mark 16:15. Christ has commissioned your church to make disciples.

You may also serve the Savior in a parachurch context. The Bible will address your mission directly or indirectly. Whatever your ministry, you should begin the mission-developing process by searching the Scriptures to determine what they say about what you want to accomplish as a ministry. If your ministry focuses on evangelism, what does the Bible say about evangelism?

2. *Whom are you attempting to serve?* A ministry must focus on people, not programs. This is because ministry is people-centered not program-centered. Since you can't reach everybody, you must ask, *Who will I reach?* (your future ministry constituency) and, *Who am I reaching?* (present ministry constituency). Both questions are essential. If your present or future ministry consists of older people, then you'll probably attract older people. If it consists of younger people, then it will attract other young people. In the latter part of the twentieth century, the majority of churches have targeted Christians and virtually ignored non-Christians. However, many new churches at the turn of the century are not only ministering to their present constituency (members), but are targeting seekers—those who are lost but interested in spiritual matters.

Most would answer the above question as to who they are trying to reach with, "our community." While that in some cases is a valid answer, many who attend the church may not live in its community. The parish system in North America is dead. Consequently, another answer might be, "unchurched people." To target churched people is to steal sheep. Should you practice this, you and your church will be very unpopular with other churches in the area. Instead, why not target unchurched people, both lost and saved, outside your community as well as in it. You may not wish to include whom you're attempting to serve in your mission statement and that's okay. Regardless, you need to answer the question.

3. *How will you minister to people?* The final question gets at the nature of your ministry to people. It asks the following: What are you going to do for people? What services will you provide for them? Will you attempt to win people to Christ and lead Christians to a deeper walk with Christ? If you are a church, then you are to attempt an even balance between the two. Parachurch ministries have an easier time knowing how they will minister to people because they begin with a specific ministry service in mind such as evangelism, discipleship, stewardship, and others.

What does a good mission statement look like? The following example for a fictitious church answers well the above questions:

> The mission of Grace Church is to lead the people of southern Collin County to faith in Christ and growth in Christlikeness.

Answering the first question of determining what you're supposed to be doing according to the Scriptures will always be easy. This is obviously a church ministry because its mission is the Great Commission. Though not necessary, it clearly designates whom it will serve—the people of southern Collin County. It also clarifies how it will serve them—it will lead them to faith in Christ and growth in Christlikeness.

Step 2: Articulate Your Mission in a Written Statement

The next step in developing your mission is to get it down on paper. According to my definition, a mission is a statement of what your ministry is supposed to be doing. The power of the mission statement is that it's written, not spoken. Writing the mission statement blows the cobwebs off the brain. It forces you to clarify and focus your thinking about your mission. If you know it, you can write it down. There are several miniquestions that will help you to take this second step.

1. *What words communicate best with your people?* It takes some time to write a good mission statement. The mission drafters will need to shape and reshape, draft and redraft the statement until it's just right. Much of this shaping and drafting involves its wording, involves personalizing the mission. You want to choose the words that best fit your people and to some degree your target audience. (The mission statement is primarily for your people.) Old familiar clichés turn off a younger audience, whereas, fresh contemporary terms attract them.

A demographic study of your present or target audience will provide you with the information you need to make these determinations. A demographic study equips you with information such as people's education, marital status, employment, number of children, and so on. If you are presently in a ministry, then much of this information will be at your fingertips. I've noticed, however, that a number of ministries tend to ignore demographic studies—to their disadvantage; thus they lose touch with their people. If you are starting a new ministry, a number of professional organizations will provide this kind of information.[1] You may also wish to conduct your own congregational and community surveys.

You should also be aware of terms that are regional and limited to a particular part of the country. It's not wrong to use these terms. The warning is to make sure that your terms fit the region. Terms that make sense in Dallas, Texas, a distinct part of the South, might not make sense in New England. The following is a mission statement developed by Colonial Chapel in Connecticut.

> Colonial Chapel exists to colonize Connecticut and the greater commonwealth with citizens of Heaven who possess a new spiritual constitution, who passionately embrace the revolutionary teachings of Jesus Christ, who have declared themselves "in dependence" upon God, His word and His people, and whose mission is to proclaim the truth which sets men free, liberating them from the rule of darkness.

The pastor has spent time carefully crafting and redrafting this statement to find the precise words for his ministry constituency. He uses words such as *commonwealth*, *constitution*, and *revolutionary* that are commonplace in New England but might seem out of place in some other region of the country.

2. *Do your people understand what you've written?* This raises the issue of clarity. If people don't understand your mission statement, then you don't have one! Christian ministries tend to use biblical terms in their mission statements. The problem is that, according to a Gallup poll, most Americans are biblically illiterate, and this has proved true in churches as well.

One popular word that has caused some clarity problems is *disciple*. It has proved problematic not only for the public in general but also for the Christian community in particular. The question is, *What is a disciple?* Consequently, some churches have used words that define the word *disciple* for their audience. One example is the mission statement of Willow Creek Community Church:

> The mission of Willow Creek Community Church is to turn irreligious people into fully devoted followers of Jesus Christ.

Willow Creek could have said that they desire to turn irreligious people into disciples. But what does that mean for their people—many of whom are former seekers who are just learning about their new faith? So Willow Creek opted for "fully devoted followers of Christ."

Another example is the mission statement of a church I pastored, Northwood Community Church in Dallas, Texas.

> Our mission is to develop people into fully functioning followers of Christ.

We also wrestled with the problematic word *disciple*. Our solution was to substitute the words "fully functioning followers of Christ." To the casual reader or leader, this may sound trivial; however, it could make the difference in people's understanding and in implementing your ministry's mission. At Northwood, we define a fully functioning follower as one who is characterized by the three *c*s: conversion, commitment, and contribution. A fully functioning follower has been converted to Christ, has committed his or her life to Christ, and is contributing to the cause of Christ.

3. *Does your mission format convey your mission statement well?* Your mission statement may take any one of a number of forms. The only limitation might be your creative abilities. Three primary formats characterize most of the mission statements in my collection.

Format #1 looks like this:

The mission of (name of your ministry) is to

_____

An example is the statement of the fictional Crossroads Church of Oklahoma City, Oklahoma:

The mission of Crossroads Church is to win the lost and empower believers to become fully functioning followers of Christ.

This format is simple and gets to the point. Its disadvantage, however, is that it's formal and lacks a personal touch.

Format #2 looks like this:

(Name of your ministry)
Our mission is to _____

If Crossroads Church had adopted this format, it would look like the following:

Crossroads Church
Our mission is to win the lost and empower believers to become fully functioning followers of Christ.

This format has all the advantages of the first—it's simple and straightforward. The use of the personal pronoun "our" adds a personal touch.

Format #3 looks like this:

(Name of your ministry) seeks to _____

_____

Had Crossroads Church chosen this format, it would look like this:

Crossroads Church seeks to win the lost and empower believers to become fully functioning followers of Christ.

This format has all the advantages of the first. If you don't like the word *seeks*, you might choose to use some other verb such as *desires, aspires, aims, strives*, or *exists*. Format #3 also has some potential disadvantages. One is that it seems a little formal as does format #1. The second is that you might not know that it's a mission statement because it doesn't tell you what it is.

You have already noted that each format follows its verb with an infinitive. In the above example from Crossroads Church, the verb *seeks* is followed by the infinitive *to win* and the implied infinitive *to empower*. Choose the exact infinitive very carefully—not just any infinitive will do. The key is what you hope to accomplish for your target audience. You have already determined this in your answer to the third miniquestion of step one. Here are some infinitives that might prove helpful:

To assist	To create	To craft	To convert
To develop	To empower	To energize	To equip

| To establish | To help | To lead | To prepare |
| To produce | To promote | To provide | To share |

Step 3: Strike a Balance Between Breadth and Clarity

Step three asks you to find the balance between breadth and clarity. They might appear to be opposites—the broader the statement, the less clear it is. The two, however, can coexist in dynamic tension. You want the mission statement to be both broad and clear at the same time. The temptation for most mission developers is to err to one extreme or the other. Your job is to land in between. Two miniquestions will help you do this.

1. *Is your mission statement broad enough?* The first element in the definition of a mission is breadth. Since most ministries conduct multiple functions, such as Christian education, small groups, worship, evangelism, and others, your statement should be broad enough to include all that you're doing in your ministry. Also, if a ministry function doesn't fit under your mission statement, either the statement isn't broad enough or the ministry function goes beyond the scope of your mission and you should jettison it. For example, a number of churches have decided to start Christian schools and some have planted Christian colleges. The question for you is, Is a Christian school a part of our mission statement? Does it fall under the mission umbrella? If not, then don't start one.

2. *Is your mission statement clear?* The danger with the first miniquestion is that a statement can become so broad that it doesn't say anything. As you work through the process, ask yourself and others, *What specifically does this mean?*

There are some words that mask ministry clarity. For example, some ministries will use the word *glory* as in "the glory of God" or "the glory of Christ." It appears in a statement that says the church desires to glorify God in some way. How can anyone object to such a term since it's biblical? The problem is, *What does it mean specifically?* Instead, use a different word such as honor and then go on to explain how, specifically, you will honor or glorify God.

Another way to ensure mission clarity is to include a separate statement that provides further clarification, even though this could be awkward and burdensome.

A test of mission clarity is the "people test." The mission statement is primarily an in-house document. It is written for your people and for those outside the ministry who might be interested in becoming a part of the ministry. (It's not for the lost people whom you're attempting to reach with the gospel.) Therefore, you should quiz your people. Ask them what the mission draft communicates to them. When it passes the people test, then you have achieved mission clarity.

Step 4: Keep It Brief and Simple

Step four focuses on brevity that leads to simplicity. Brevity walks hand in hand with simplicity. The second element in my definition of a fully functional mission is that it is brief. The following four miniquestions will help you to accomplish this end.

1. *Have you committed information overload?* A characteristic of some who develop a mission is that they attempt to include too much in the statement. To achieve clarity, they want to pack as much information as possible into the product. Actually, this serves only to confuse those who need to understand and carry out the ministry's mission. People can handle only so much information. Consequently, we must include less, not more, in our statements. Information overload is the enemy, not the friend, of clarity.

I have observed that information overload masks itself in three basic forms. The first is to include a definition or explanation of the ministry in the mission statement. The following is a fictitious example:

The mission of Hartford Divinity School as a professional, graduate-level school is to train future ministers to lead our denomination of churches.

The statement, "as a professional, graduate-level school," is a definition or explanation. It defines or explains who the Hartford Divinity School is. While this is important, it need not be in the mission statement. It qualifies as information overload. If the statement is in the school's catalog, then it's probably understood and not necessary. Otherwise, it might appear in a separate statement. Dropping the definition makes it more simple: The mission of Hartford Divinity School is to train future ministers to lead our denomination of churches.

A second form of overload is to include the strategy for accomplishing your mission or parts of your mission in the mission statement. This is the most common form of information overload that I have come across in working with churches. The following is an invented example:

> The mission of Grace Bible Church is to lead our people to growth in Christlikeness by equipping them through the exposition of God's Word for ministry in the twenty-first century.

The entire statement, "by equipping them through the exposition of God's Word for ministry in the twenty-first century," is strategy. It explains not what but how. It is, in fact, important that people know how you plan to accomplish your mission—so important that it should appear in a strategy statement separate from the mission statement. To include it with the mission makes the latter needlessly complex. Phrases introduced by prepositions such as *by* and *through* are red flags that signal complexity when they are tacked onto the mission statement.

A third form of information overload is to include both a definition and the strategy in the same statement with the mission. This is the worst and most confusing form of overload:

> The mission of Hartford Divinity School as a professional, graduate-level school is to train future ministers to lead our denomination of churches by blending sociological studies and modern theological principles with training in ministry skills.

As before, the explanation or definition comes after the name of the school and is signaled by the word *as*. The prepositions *by* and *with* come at the end of the statement and signal strategy. The mission would be much simpler if these were dropped, revealing the mission statement itself: The mission of Hartford Divinity School is to train future ministers to lead our denomination of churches.

2. *Does your statement pass the T-shirt test?* The power of the mission statement is in its brevity and simplicity. Peter Drucker is correct when he says that a good mission statement should be short enough to fit on a T-shirt. It would be difficult to place the inflated, overloaded mission statement for Hartford Divinity School on a T-shirt. Even if you could, the letters would have to be so small that you might have difficulty reading it. The statement from Willow Creek, "our mission is to turn irreligious people into fully devoted followers of Christ," would fit on any T-shirt. The same is true of Pantego Bible Church's mission: "To transform people, through the work of the Holy Spirit, into fully developing followers of Christ."

3. *Can you express your mission in one sentence?* The best, most powerful mission statements are simple, one-sentence statements. They get right to the point. Note the power of each of the following mission statement sentences:

> Our mission is to transform people, through the work of the Holy Spirit, into fully developing followers of Christ.
>
> —Pantego Bible Church

> Our mission is to attack the enemy and defeat him.
>
> —United States Marine Corps

> Our mission is to make citizens out of the rejected.
>
> —The Salvation Army

Our mission is to prepare men and women for ministry in the local churches.

—Winebrenner Theological Seminary

4. *Is your mission easily remembered?* Our goal as leaders is to provide our people with a mission statement that is both easily understood and remembered. It should have staying power; it should stick to the ribs of one's mind. You don't want your people to attempt to memorize it. You want people to hear it several times and remember it naturally. This won't happen if you try to cram too much information into the statement or include an explanation of your ministry or your strategy. People simply won't put forth the mental effort that it takes to remember it. The case in point as being memorable is the four one-sentence mission statements above. A few moments have elapsed since you read them. Can you remember any of them? Chances are excellent that if you read over them several times, even though there are four, you would remember them due to their succinctness and power. Though it doesn't appear above, my all-time favorite is "to know Christ and make Him known" and "to present Christ as Savior and pursue Christ as Lord."

QUESTIONS FOR REFLECTION, DISCUSSION, AND APPLICATION

1. Who will write your mission statement? Why? Is this person responsible for initiating and completing the process? How many other people will be involved in this project? Who are they? Will you enlist the help of a consultant?

2. Are you and the other leaders in your ministry convinced that you need a clear, biblical mission? Why or why not? Have they taken the ministry mission audit (see page 68)? If yes, what did you learn from the audit?

3. Is the ministry ready to develop a mission? If yes, how do you know? If no, is it for the reasons mentioned in this chapter (busyness, hopelessness)? If not, then why?

4. How much time will it take for you to develop your mission statement? Do you anticipate any delays or interruptions? If so, what are they? Have you allowed for and encouraged some reflective time between meetings?

5. Where will you meet and why? Is it the best site for your team? How much will it cost? Is cost a big factor in your decision?

6. Work through the mission development process as summarized in appendix E. What is your mission? Are you happy with it? Explain. Are the others happy with it? Why or why not? Does it need some more work?

7. Do you already have a mission statement? What is it? Use the mission development process as a test of its quality. Is it a good one or does it need some more work?

Part 3

The Vision of Your Ministry

6

The Definition of Vision, Part 1

What Is a Vision?

ow that you have a biblical mission statement, next comes the crafting of a biblical vision. You need to decide what God's vision is for your church. This has been problematic for the North American church. Writing in *Leadership*, David Goetz states, "In *Leadership's* study, however, pastors indicated that *conflicting visions for the church* was their greatest source of tension and the top reason they were terminated or forced to resign."[1] George Barna writes of pastors that "only 2% could articulate the vision for their church . . . that's one reason so many pastors are ineffective; they don't know where they're going."[2]

Both mission and vision are important for essentially the same reasons; however, some confusion exists over the definition of a vision. If your church's leadership is to develop a compelling vision, it needs to know what a vision is. What is it you're attempting to do? What kinds of visions are there? How is a vision different from a mission? This chapter will answer the first two questions, thus defining and determining an organizational, ministry vision. Chapter 7 will answer the third question by delineating the differences between a mission and a vision. Finally, chapter 8 will guide you in developing a clear, compelling vision for your ministry.

THE DEFINITION OF A VISION

I define an organizational vision as a clear, challenging picture of God's vision for the ministry as it can and must be. This definition includes six critical elements.

A Vision Is Clear

The first element of a vision is clarity. It's difficult to accomplish what you don't know. A leader without a clear vision has much in common with a person trying to drive blindfolded. I spent one summer pastoring a seeker church, Crossroads Community Church in Amsterdam, Holland. Since we were so close to France, one weekend my wife and I traveled south to Paris. While there, we visited the Arc de Triomphe—a massive, imposing structure that serves as a hub for a number of streets that come together in the heart of Paris. Each street empties into a single street that circles the Arc de Triomphe. You could easily spot the native Parisians, as opposed to the tourists, who attempted to navigate the circular, one-way street. Traffic was constantly attempting to either get on or off the street. For the tourists it was a nightmare. They must have felt that they were on a merry-go-round and couldn't get off. It would have been utter foolishness for a Parisian much less a tourist to attempt to navigate the circle wearing a blindfold.

I believe that a person who attempts to lead a ministry without a vision will have an experience similar to a blindfolded tourist attempting to drive around the Arc de Triomphe. In today's world, the only constant, except for the Scriptures, is change. We live in a century wherein everything is changing at breakneck speed. Navigating a ministry vehicle through the last decade of the twentieth century and beyond will prove impossible unless everyone on board knows where that vehicle is headed.

Some ministries do have a vision. The Barna estimate cited previously sets the number of pastors with a vision at 2 percent. But how many of the people in their churches know and understand that vision? If the people who make up a ministry don't understand the vision, then it's not clear. And if it's not clear, then you don't have a vision.

How clear does the vision need to be? I ask pastors what kind of response I would get if I paid an unannounced visit to their church on Sunday morning and asked people what the vision of the church is. I suspect that far too many wouldn't know what I was talking about. Most would refer me back to the pastor. It would be insightful, then, for pastors who have what they think is a clear vision to conduct a vision-clarity test. This involves randomly asking people, including the leaders, what the church's vision is. If the response is silence or a puzzled look, then your vision isn't clear and your work is cut out for you.

Most churches thirst for a biblical vision. I spoke recently with a lay leader of a small church that was without a pastor. Vision was at the top of their list of what they were looking for in a new pastor. Because this church desperately needed clear direction, they were looking for a pastor who was a visionary. While the mission statement provides a ministry with direction, it's the vision statement that creates a clear picture of that direction.

God gave Moses both a clear mission and a clear vision. The mission is found in Exodus 3:10: "So now, go. I am sending you to Pharaoh to bring my people the Israelites out of Egypt." This was preceded by Moses' vision in Exodus 3:7–8: "The LORD said, 'I have indeed seen the misery of my people in Egypt. I have heard them crying out because of their slave drivers, and I am concerned about their suffering. So I have come down to rescue them from the hand of the Egyptians and to bring them up out of that land into a good and spacious land, a land flowing with milk and honey—the home of the Canaanites, Hittites, Amorites, Perizzites, Hivites and Jebusites.'" The issue for Moses wasn't vision clarity; it was his confidence in his competence to do that which God had made clear to him (Exod. 3:11).

A Vision Is Challenging

The second element of a vision is that it challenges people. In the Middle Ages, knights wore a flexible metal glove to protect their hands from injury during battle. They called this glove a gauntlet. If the knight wished to challenge someone to personal combat or to express defiance over some issue, it was customary to throw down or take up his gauntlet. This is what a vision does for leaders. It enables them to challenge their people to accomplish great things for the Savior. In short, it inspires or motivates them. This is crucial at a time in North America during which far too many leaders envision throwing in the towel, not throwing down a gauntlet.

It's my firm conviction that pastoring a church is one of the most leadership-intensive tasks that a person could attempt in today's world. This is due primarily to the church's nature as a voluntary, nonprofit organization. It's difficult enough trying to lead people in for-profit organizations. The typical leader has very little leverage in a church because it is a nonprofit ministry that depends heavily on volunteers to conduct so much of the ministry.

So, how do you challenge these people? Military leaders can issue orders and marketplace leaders can pay handsomely for people's services. The church has no such leverage. The key is motivating people, and the key to motivation is a clear, challenging vision. Consequently, ministries without a vision are in trouble for there is little else that motivates people to give their lives in service for Christ.

At the end of the 1980s, I was reflecting on the vision concept and working with a few churches in the area of vision development. The first church with whom I conducted a vision seminar taught me an important lesson. We spent what we thought was a productive weekend at a comfortable home on a large lake located near Dallas, Texas. We started on Friday evening and finished up Saturday afternoon. Most important was that we had a vision statement to show for all our hard work. One of the leaders had written it down on paper. The task-oriented leadership board was pleased because they had accomplished their goal for the weekend—the development of a church vision statement. The only problem was that when they returned to the church, they filed the vision statement in the church filing cabinet somewhere under *v* and promptly forgot it.

While this church had a so-called vision on paper, they had no vision in practice. The presence of a written document in a filing cabinet "does not a vision make." A good vision challenges the vision designers and the people for whom it's intended. If they're not inspired to implement a God-honoring vision, then they don't have a vision. The document serves only to fill up much-needed space in some church filing cabinet—it challenges and motivates no one.

God's vision for Israel motivated and challenged them. They were in bondage to Egypt. The Egyptians were cruel taskmasters. So cruel that Moses killed one Egyptian because he was beating a Hebrew (Exod. 2:11–13). Then Moses came to Israel with a message of God's freedom and redemption: "And I have promised to bring you up out of your misery in Egypt into the land of the Canaanites, Hittites, Amorites, Perizzites, Hivites and Jebusites—a land flowing with milk and honey" (Exod. 3:17). There was a stark contrast between the harsh condition of making bricks for slave masters in a foreign land and living in your own land that overflowed with milk and honey. Once Moses cast God's vision for his people, they were so challenged that they bowed down and worshipped God (Exod. 4:31).

A Vision Is a Picture

The third vital element is that a vision is a mental picture. As passion is a "feeling" word, so vision is a "seeing" word. In his foreword to my *Developing a Vision for Ministry in the Twenty-first Century*, Haddon Robinson tells the story of someone who, shortly after the completion of Disney World, said to Mike Vance, the director of Disney Studios, "Isn't it too bad that Walt Disney didn't live to see this!" To which the director replied, "He did see it—that's why it's here."[3]

One of my former students sent me a cartoon that illustrates this point well. The title for the cartoon is "Frog Pioneers." It consists of three frogs wearing coonskin hats and with shovels resting on their shoulders. They're standing in the middle of a desert next to a giant cactus. The caption above one frog's head reads, "We'll put the swamp here!" I like to show this cartoon to people and ask them what they see. Most see the frogs and the cactus. The vision question, however, is, "What do the *frogs* see?" A vision paints a picture of what tomorrow will look like. Your vision for your ministry is what you see in your head when you close your eyes and picture your ministry two, five, ten, even twenty years from now.

Visionary leaders have a mental picture of what the transcendent, contemporary God has in mind for his people today. They carry in their mental billfolds a visual snapshot of what God can do in their ministries. When they walk through a community, whether located in the throes of poverty in the inner city or the spate of new homes in the suburbs, they don't see just houses or people. They see opportunities for the Savior. They envision places where they can plant churches, and people to whom they can minister.

As a seminary professor, I have the privilege of training seminarians as future leaders. As a pastor and church consultant, I also have the honor of training pastors and leadership teams in the context of their ministries. Much of this training is in the area of leadership in general and vision development in particular. Leaders need to take time out of their schooling or busy ministries and dream about the future. They are to picture in their minds what God can do in and through them. As various pictures and images come to mind, I encourage them to write them down.

Not every person is a visionary. God has created some to be visionaries and others to be practical realists. The body of Christ needs both. The visionaries are the more intuitive people who focus on future ideas and what could be, while realists are those who focus on present reality and what is. Those who would lead ministries from the point position should be visionaries. Those who aren't visionaries usually function best in a support position.

You can find out which you are by taking the Myers-Briggs Type Indicator (MBTI) test. It has two preferences that represent both of the above. The intuitive is the visionary; the sensing is the nonvisionary. I should add that while sensing-type people are not natural visionaries, this doesn't mean that they can't catch a vision. They just have to go about doing it a different way because it doesn't come naturally to them; they have to go and see the vision to grasp it. For example, if you're a visionary pastor with a nonvisionary board, then you'll need to take these people to visit a church that has your same vision. They will literally see the vision through their own eyes and hear it through their ears and come to understand what you've been saying.

An important aspect of God's vision for Israel was that they could see their future in the Promised Land. It was to be a future of prosperity—a land flowing with milk and honey. God used his servant Moses to cast and recast this vision throughout the Pentateuch. In one such incident in Deuteronomy 8:7–9, the picture of their future is even more graphic. Moses says, "For the LORD your God is bringing you into a good land—a land with streams and pools of water, with springs flowing in the valleys and hills; a land with wheat and barley, vines and fig trees, pomegranates, olive oil and honey; a land where bread will not be scarce and you will lack nothing; a land where the rocks are iron and you can dig copper out of the hills." The purpose was to provide the Israelites with a mental picture of what their future life would be like.

A Vision Is God's Future for the Ministry

The fourth element of vision is that it concerns the future. It's a clear description of God's preferred future for your ministry. It's a mental picture of what tomorrow will look like. It depicts the kind of ministry that he desires yours to become. It's an expression of all your God inspired hopes and dreams for your church or parachurch ministry. Therefore, when you develop an organizational vision for your ministry, you are thinking about its future.

The older, traditional churches of North America aren't doing well at the end of the twentieth century and the beginning of the third millennium. Lyle Schaller indicates that "two thirds to three fourths of all congregations founded before 1960 are either on a plateau in size or shrinking in numbers."[4] One of the reasons for their decline is that they function as if they are living in the 1940s and 1950s. Their ministry minds are focused on the past when America was a Christian-friendly culture. Unless they change their focus and begin to envision the future, their demise is only a matter of time. You can't drive forward when you spend all your time staring in the rearview mirror. Ministry isn't about the past. We can learn from the past and celebrate the victories of the past as God's people did in the Old Testament, but we're not to live in the past as so many of these churches are attempting to do. Ministry takes place in the present and is predicated on the future.

Except for biblical prophecy, the future cannot be predicted. You can, however, predetermine the future. You determine your future and that of your ministry by creating it. This involves the realization and development of all the potential that God has placed at your ministry's fingertips. It involves making the best choices from all the many ministry possibilities and probabilities that lie before you, but the cultivation of a clear organizational vision is a vital determiner in creating and influencing the future of your ministry. It spells out what kind of ministry you plan to be and inspires your people to accomplish it.

Christ has already predetermined his preferred future for the church. He has already defined what the church is supposed to accomplish in this world—the Great Commission. The present and future ministry of the church is to make disciples (Matt. 28:19). The mission of the church and the vision of the church are the same—the Great Commission. The difference is that the vision is what you see as the church realizes its mission in the ministry community.

It's the nature of a vision that it always lives in the future. When an organization accomplishes a vision, then it's over and done with. An example is God's vision for Israel. As long as Moses and the people were wandering in the wilderness, he would cast and recast their dream because it was in the future. Once they arrived in the land, the vision was accomplished.

God's vision for Israel through Moses was a short-term vision. The vision was realized. It had an end. Long-term visions are different. They're perpetually in a state of becoming and are open-ended. The Great Commission is a long-term vision. It involves pursuing and winning lost people and then leading them as new Christians to Christlikeness. The desire is that each and every church will win many people for the Savior. As Christ said, however, the harvest is great, therefore, the church will never fully accomplish this vision. The paradoxical is, then, the church is accomplishing what it can't fully accomplish.

A Vision Can Be

The fifth element is feasibility. A good vision is feasible. It exists in the realm of possibility. It concerns not "what is" but "what can be." The visionary dream often begins with a deep dissatisfaction with the status quo—it's unacceptable—and a clear grasp of and desire for a better alternative. President John F. Kennedy summed it up well when he said, "Some people see things the way they are and ask why; I see things the way they could be and ask why not?"

In my ministry of teaching and consulting, I find that most ministries err in one of two directions concerning feasibility. The first is that the majority think too small; they have little or no vision. This is often true of seminarians. When they complete their studies, they tend to think too small about their future ministries. One reason is that so many have little ministry experience before coming to seminary, and they spend their time in seminary primarily in the classroom or the library. Thus, they aren't sure of their ministry competence. They ask, *Can I lead? Can I preach? Can I do ministry well?* When one questions his or her competence, this adversely affects confidence and diminishes vision.

I find that things aren't that different in the actual ministry world. The churches sprinkled all across North America are going though a period of change. Many small churches are dying while the larger churches are growing bigger. The old-timers in the small churches are hanging in there in spite of the changing communities all around. Their children, however, aren't proving as faithful. Many attend the larger churches with broader ministry menus and more to offer their kids. If you ask the faithful about their church's vision, their response is, "Huh? We're just trying to keep the doors open!"

This isn't anything new to the ministry world. In Ephesians 3:20, Paul appears to give the first-century church at Ephesus a slap on the wrist for a lack of vision. At the end of his benediction that begins in verse 14, he says, "Now to Him who is able to do far more abundantly beyond all that we ask or think . . ." (NASB). He seems to be mildly scolding them for not asking big enough or thinking big enough. This raises the obvious question, *What are you praying for and what do you envision? How big are your prayers and dreams?*

The Savior was impressed by men and women of strong faith. In Matthew 8, a centurion asked Jesus to heal his servant. This was a man with much power under the Roman military system, who believed, however, that he was unworthy of Jesus' presence (v. 8). His humble request was that Jesus simply speak because he was convinced that his words would heal his servant. Matthew records the Savior's response in verse 10: "When Jesus heard this, he was astonished and said to those following him, 'I tell you the truth, I have not found anyone in Israel with such great faith.'"

Jesus periodically rebuked the disciples for not having enough faith. On one occasion, the disciples were worried about their daily need of food and clothing (Matt. 6:25–34). He sadly responds to their lack of trust with the words, "Oh you of little faith" (v. 30). This response is important because faith and vision walk hand in hand. Those with little faith most often have little vision. Those with much faith usually display much vision. Consequently, if you want to dream greater dreams, then work on your faith.

While it is rare, the other error is to think too big. The problem is that a vision can be so large that it overwhelms the people in the ministry. When a vision is too big, it intimidates people and dries up their ministry energy before they get started. A sense of futility prevails, and, in time, people drop out of the church. How can you know if your vision is too big? Consider these questions: First, who is the leader, the visionary? Is that person just out of seminary with little if any ministry experience? Is he or she a proven leader who has led other churches or ministries with high impact? Second, who are the followers? Are these people capable of realizing the vision? It's not the leader but his or her followers who carry out the vision. Do these people have the necessary training, gifts, and desire to realize the vision? Finally, is the time right for this vision? Some leaders are way out in front of the times. They anticipate the future so far in advance that the culture or the ministry isn't yet ready for their visions. Other leaders may have fallen behind the times. The world has passed them by and they don't know it. A third group are on top of the times. Like the men of Issachar in the Old Testament, they know how to exegete the culture and are aware of what is taking place around them and how to minister to people (1 Chron. 12:32).

A Vision Must Be

The sixth element is a critical sense of urgency. Not only does the visionary believe that the vision can be, he or she is convinced that it must be. It's more than feasible; the future and, in some cases, the survival of the ministry depend on it.

What fuels this sense of urgency in the visionary? The answer is passion. The visionary is passionate over the vision. He or she feels very strongly about it. The disparity between what is and what could be ignites a passion in the leader's heart. It compels him or her to turn this vision into reality. Ken Hemphill, a seminary president, writes, "Vision is not what ignites growth, it's passion. Burden creates passion. Passion fuels vision, and vision is the focus of the power of passion. I've discovered in churches that leaders who are passionate about their calls create vision."[5]

Several variables contribute to this passion for the vision. One is that God is behind it. He is the source and he is responsible for it. It's his vision for this time and this ministry. Nehemiah sensed this when in Nehemiah 2:12 he says, "I did not tell anyone what my God was putting into my mind to do for Jerusalem" (NASB). Another is a sense that God has raised you up to lead with this dream. Like King David in his generation, you are here to serve God's purpose in this your generation (see Acts 13:36). A third is that the culture and the ministry desperately need this vision. The future of the ministry and the survival of the culture ultimately depend on it.

The definition of a vision, as put forth in this chapter, helps you to understand what a vision is. It also serves as a test for an existing or a newly developed vision. Despite the lack of a vision on the part of most churches, some ministries do have one. Others are in the process of discovering and developing what they believe is God's vision for their ministries. How can you know if your vision is a good one? The vision audit below functions as a template or guide to measure whether the old or new vision is a good one or needs some work.

Vision Audit

1. Is your vision clear? Do the people who are a part of your ministry understand the vision? Can they articulate it? Does it pass the "people test"?

2. Is the dream challenging? Does it excite people? Does it move people to action?

3. Does the vision create a picture in people's minds? Can they see your dream?

4. Is your dream future oriented? Does it create a picture of the preferred future that God desires for your ministry? Does it give everyone an idea of what lies ahead?

5. Do you believe that this dream can be? Given who you are and your ministry circumstances, is it feasible?

6. Are you convinced that it must be? Do you feel strongly about this vision? Has it touched you emotionally? Will your ministry or your community be better for it?

A VISION ON VARIOUS LEVELS

In defining the mission statement in chapter 4, I included a discussion of the various kinds of mission statements and focused as well on personal, organizational, and departmental missions. Each adds to our understanding of the mission concept. The same is true for the vision. An understanding of the kinds of visions will further clarify a vision. I present the vision in the same three categories.

Personal Vision

Chapter 4 encourages you to develop a personal mission statement for your life. That mission statement will determine what you'll do with your life. It's a succinct statement that helps you focus your energies in a way that best serves Christ. When various opportunities for ministry come along, the mission statement also serves as a template or guide for decision making. If the opportunity lines up with your personal mission, then you should carefully consider whether God is moving you in a new direction. If it doesn't, then you have your answer.

Where does personal vision fit into all this? Your personal vision is different from your mission. The mission statement logically precedes the vision statement. Your personal vision is what you see when you envision the realization of your mission in your life and ministry. My vision statement is what I see in my head when I think about implementing my mission, which is *training a new generation of godly leaders for high-impact ministry in the twenty-first century.* My vision is what I see taking place as I travel and train young, godly men and women for ministry in this world.

Organizational Vision

I place personal vision before organizational vision. Your personal vision takes precedence. The latter must be in line with the former. If this doesn't happen, then you will find yourself working and ministering in an organization that doesn't complement who you are as a person or your direction in life. You're the proverbial fish out of water.

As with the mission concept, several terms serve to describe the organizational vision. If you minister in a church, you might call it the church's vision or a congregational vision. If you minister in either a church or parachurch context, you could refer to it as your institutional vision. You might also use the word *corporate* if your ministry is in a church, parachurch, or marketplace setting. Formally, most use the word *corporate* of any organization that is incorporated under the laws of a particular state. Informally, you may use the word *corporate* of your ministry regardless of its nature.

Departmental Vision

The departmental vision works hand in glove with the departmental mission. In chapter 4 I urged you to develop a mission for any departments that make up your ministry. Doing so serves to bring the mission concept down to the grassroots level—where the people who are at the heart of the ministry are. It shows them how what they're doing serves Christ and fits into the ministry's big picture. This will give them a strong sense of purpose and a feeling of importance. Finally, it serves to focus every department on what it's supposed to be doing as it contributes to what the ministry as a whole is doing.

You should encourage your departments to develop departmental visions. This will help them and those who might join them in ministry to envision what they're doing. Developing a departmental mission helps each to *know* specifically what they're doing and where they're going. Developing a departmental vision helps them *see* what they're doing and where they're going. A departmental vision statement paints a mental picture of what their departments will look like as they realize their individual missions, which will strongly challenge and inspire them to be intentional about accomplishing their dreams for the future.

7

The Definition of Vision, Part 2

What Is the Difference Between a Vision and a Mission?

This book recognizes an obvious, clear distinction between vision and mission; it treats them separately in parts 2 and 3. In my work with these ideas, various leaders have asked me to clarify the differences between a vision and a mission. Consequently, I make a point in my initial presentation of the vision to detail these differences in anticipation of the question. The vision and the mission have some qualities in common and some that are distinct. The latter outnumber the former. This chapter will help pastors and other leaders understand these concepts more fully by detailing first their similarities and then their differences.

THE SIMILARITIES BETWEEN A VISION AND A MISSION

The vision and mission have no less than four common elements. Both find their source in God. Both are future focused. And both are direction oriented. Both are function directed. Most likely you as a reader sensed this much as you worked through the prior mission and vision material. Let's examine these similarities more closely.

Vision and Mission Are Sourced in God

The first common element is that both the vision and the mission must come from God. You are to seek God's mission and dream for your ministry, not your own. Thus, leaders must determine and articulate God's will for these two areas.

Some seek to know God's desires for their lives and ministries through means such as dreams and supernatural visions, such as Peter's in Acts 10:9–22, Isaiah's in Isaiah 6, and Daniel's in Daniel 7. Who are we to say that God can't work this way today? The problem, however, is that it's difficult to separate that which is legitimate from that which is false. We have learned the need for knowing the difference from David Koresh and the Branch Davidian group who followed Koresh's false vision to their deaths in Waco, Texas. But this is not a new lesson. We learned it once before from Jim Jones who led a group of the disenchanted to follow his vision to their deaths in Guyana in South America.

A sure source for determining God's will is that it is verifiable in the Scriptures. God's will is found in his Word. God has predetermined the mission and to some extent the vision of the church. The church's mission is clearly the Great Commission. Christ has instructed his followers to make disciples (Matt. 28:19; Mark 16:15). The church's vision grows out of this mission, though it is one step beyond the mission. Vision involves envisioning what the realization of the Great Commission mission will look like as Christ's disciples implement it in their distinct ministry communities. Therefore, you find both in God's Word.

The parachurch ministry, too, should find its source, to some extent, for vision and mission in God's Word. Most of these ministries spring out of a biblical exhortation to evangelize the lost, build up the saved, help the family, or lift up the disenfranchised or downtrodden. This would characterize the ministries of organizations such as Campus Crusade for Christ, the Navigators, Focus on the Family, the Salvation Army, and various Christian rescue missions.

Vision and Mission Are Future Focused

The development and articulation of a mission makes a statement about a ministry's future. Crafting the mission defines and determines the ministry's future, but the ministry's past can also be helpful in addressing the mission. The past serves as a teacher. We can learn from our past failures as well as our victories, and these speak to our future direction. The problem occurs when a church or parachurch organization decides to camp in the past. Ministry has taken place in the past, but that's history. Now ministry can no longer take place in the past. It's always done in the present with a view toward the future, and that future is the overall goal or mission.

The vision statement also has everything to do with a ministry's future. Whereas the mission statement makes a declaration about a ministry's future, the vision statement provides a picture of what that future will look like. Again, vision is a *seeing* word. It isn't enough that your ministry constituency knows where they are going, they should be able to see where they are going. That's a primary function of the vision as it's cast before the people. It provides a window through which all can see the church's tomorrow.

Vision and Mission Are Direction Oriented

One of the more important questions that an organization can ask itself is, *Where are we going?* This is the *direction* question. The mission is directional. The *Christian* organization must ask, *Where does God want us to go*? Many of our North American churches either don't know or have forgotten the answer to that question. They aren't going anywhere. They simply exist. They're alive for the sake of being alive. Often a group of faithful old-timers is keeping their local denominational church alive because it would seem like such a travesty to see it die. Over the years, they have invested much time and money in the work, but when you ask why, many shrug their shoulders and begin to talk about all their memories. Churches such as these are directionless—without a mission or vision from God. And without both, they'll go nowhere. The tragedy is that they don't seem to know what is missing or that they even need a mission or vision. Ultimately, they miss God's direction for their church.

A vital missing element in these situations is leadership. I define a Christian leader as a godly person who knows where he or she is going and who has followers. The first quality in a leader is godliness. Christian leaders must have Christlike characters. The last quality is an ability to attract followers. If no one follows a so-called leader, then he or she isn't a leader. It's the middle quality, however, that is germane to this similarity between vision and mission. Christian leaders knows where they are going. They must have a clear sense of direction both for themselves and for their ministries. Intelligent followers want to know where they're going. Few people take a trip on a plane or a cruise on a ship without a destination clearly stamped on their tickets. The same holds true for Christians who would follow or lead others.

Both the vision statement and the mission statement provide that sense of direction. The mission statement describes the destination. Like a brochure lying on the desk in a travel agency, it tells those planning a trip where they're going. People in a church can read it on the cover of a bulletin or on a wallet-sized card or mounted on a wall plaque in the foyer. The vision statement shows people the destination. Like a poster on an agency's wall, it provides a picture. The people in the ministry can see its vision in a sermon, in the life of its leaders, or in a well-prepared video.

Vision and Mission Are Function Directed

Both a ministry's vision and its mission are function directed. They address and answer the critical *function* question: What does God want us to do? The mission is a statement of the church or parachurch organization's function. Thus, for the local church that mission is quite clear—make disciples. Whether the church understands its function or not, it still remains the same—to move people to Christlikeness. That's what is involved in making disciples. It must function in such a way that individuals move from wherever they are—lost or saved—to where God wants them to be—mature and Christlike.

Whereas the mission for the church is a statement of the function of disciple making, the vision provides a picture of what a disciple looks like. Laypeople are delighted to have a mission statement. They know that you can't focus on fog, and the mission statement blows away the fog so that they can know where the home port or final destination is. But they also want to know what a disciple looks like. What are the behavioral traits of an authentic disciple? And it's the vision, not the mission, that answers this question.

THE DIFFERENCES BETWEEN A VISION AND A MISSION

Now that we've discovered the similarities between the vision and mission, it's time to look at how they are different. I focus attention on twelve major distinctions (see chart 7.1).

The Definition

One difference between the mission and vision is found in the definition. You'll recall from chapter 4 that I defined the mission as a broad, brief, biblical statement of what God wants you to accomplish. A key, distinguishing word is *statement*. It is the crucial noun of the definition because it takes several modifiers such as broad, brief, and biblical. The phrase *of what God wants you to accomplish* is also a modifier. Consequently, you see how strategic and crucial *statement* is to the definition. It is a declaration, an expression, or a clarification of the ministry's function.

The vision is different from the mission. In chapter 6 I defined the vision as a clear, challenging picture of the future of the ministry as you believe it can and must be. A key, distinguishing term in the definition of vision is *picture*. It is a key word that is strategic to the definition. The vision is a mental picture, not a statement, of the ministry's direction and function. It's a snapshot that those in the ministry may carry in their mental purses and wallets. It's a portrait of all that God intends the church or parachurch organization to be. And it's the leader's responsibility as a gifted artist to paint for his or her people that portrait.

The Application

Another difference is application. The word *application* refers to the primary use of these two concepts. The primary application of the *mission* is in planning and strategy. It's vital to plan where the ministry organization is going and strategize how to get there. Application is a planning tool, and the mission should appear at the beginning of your planning document. The plan is dependent on and grows out of the overall goal stated in the mission.

Ministries that don't plan for their futures have no futures. Some argue that because change is now a constant, planning any further than five or six years ahead is futile. I agree. Today's trends and realities will be different in five years. However, don't interpret this statement to mean that you should jettison planning all together. Should you fail to plan, then you lose control of your future.

Planning in general, and strategizing in particular, is the responsibility of the senior pastor in a church or the president of a parachurch institution. Unfortunately, few seminaries and other institutions for training future leaders prepare their people for this critical function, yet it's essential to an effective ministry in the twenty-first century.

The primary application of the *vision* is communication. The mission statement communicates to some degree, but that isn't its primary function.

The mission is vital to planning where the church is going, and the vision is vital to communicating the same. It's a communication tool. It becomes the pastor's or primary leader's responsibility to communicate or mold the vision. He or she functions in a ministry as the "keeper of the vision." This involves cultivating (initiating and crafting), communicating (regularly casting and recasting), and clarifying (focusing and fine-tuning) the dream for the people.

The Length

A third distinction between the mission and the vision is length. The mission statement is shorter than the vision statement. The best mission statements are one sentence in length. And this sentence must be short enough to pass Peter Drucker's T-shirt test. (I must add this because some would attempt to pack fifteen or twenty words into one sentence.) The power of the mission statement is its brevity. The mission drafter must answer the question, *What's the briefest, most memorable, and powerful way to communicate our mission?* Mission statements that are brief and clear most powerfully communicate the direction and function of your ministry.

The vision statement is longer, usually much longer than a single sentence. It wouldn't and shouldn't pass the T-shirt test. I have noted that a number of organizations have developed single-sentence statements and have called them vision statements, but they are really mission statements. In the next chapter, I provide several vision statements from my collection as examples for study and evaluation. None of them are even close to a sentence in length. The vision statement is an expansion of the mission statement. It's what the mission statement looks like as it's lived out and realized in your church's ministry community. Because it's longer, you're able to supply some of the details and particulars that you couldn't include in the mission statement. This includes particular people, geographical areas, and possibly numbers, although the latter could appear in a mission statement.

The Purpose

A fourth difference is purpose. The purpose of a dynamic mission statement is to inform people about the ministry's direction. It lets them know where it's going. It also serves to inform people as to the ministry's function. Therefore, it answers two questions. The first is directional: Where are we going? The second is functional: What are we supposed to be doing? If people don't know where the ministry or church is headed and what its function is, then they're not likely to respond because they need information to react to. To paraphrase 1 Corinthians 14:8: If the bugler muffs the call to arms, then who will show up for the battle?

The vision statement has a different purpose. While it does inform to some degree, its primary purpose is to inspire people to pursue and follow the mission. It has the power to prompt people to performance, to do what the mission informs them to do. It's motivating. It calls forth the energy necessary to move people from information to action, from agreement to commitment. God's vision for Israel illustrates the power of the vision. When Moses first cast God's vision to his people, it motivated them to bow down and worship God (Exod. 4:30).

The Activity

A fifth distinction is the activity of the mission and vision. I use the word *activity* to refer to what takes place or what happens when your church or ministry both casts and implements its mission and vision. The activity that takes place when you implement and propagate your mission is doing—doing what you're supposed to be doing. This involves rolling up your ministry sleeves and getting up to your elbows in the ministry. Mission is tied closely to planning and strategy. These tools point toward the doing and ultimately the accomplishment of the overall mission. Since the mission of the church is the Great Commission, the mission activity is the action of making disciples and moving them to Christlikeness.

The mission helps those people who are the practical realists to under-stand what they're doing. They tend to live in and think about the world as it is. They desire to know what is actually there and what is actually happening. They perceive this world through the senses. Consequently, they see with their eyes and hear with their ears the mission statement and then implement it.

While the mission involves doing what you're supposed to be doing, vision involves *seeing* what you're supposed to be doing. Thus, the activity that occurs when you cast your vision is seeing. The ministry constituency not only knows what God wants them to do, but they can see it in their heads. The vision activity involves seeing disciples as well as making them.

The vision aids people who are the more intuitive or visionary types to understand what is taking place. They live and think about the world not as it is but as it could be. More than what is there and is happening, they desire to know what could be there and what could be happening. They understand our world through a sixth sense—ideas and thoughts that seem to flash out of nowhere. Therefore, they see the vision in their heads and then carry out what they see, much as an architect follows a blueprint. If people can't see it, it probably won't happen.

The Source

A sixth difference is source. The source of the mission is the head; it is based on the intellect. It's rational, logical, and cognitive—a "head thing." This is a situation where the head informs the heart. The intellect holds sway over the emotions. For example, to discover an organization's mission, we ask, *What does the Bible tell you to do?* This is a rational, cog-nitive exercise. It involves turning to the Scriptures and analyzing God's directions for his people. Once we have an answer to this question, we obey and act on that knowledge. And this is all very logical. It makes sense to your people.

The source of the vision, however, is the heart. Vision is grounded in the emotions more than in the intellect. It's not rational or logical, but it's emotive. You would find it difficult to explain and defend your thoughts to a rationalist. It's a "heart thing." When dealing with vision, the heart informs the head. The emotions hold sway over the intellect. This involves how we feel about what God has directed us to do. The vision helps you to feel strongly about directives such as the Great Commission. It introduces an element of passion into the logical world of obedience. You are moved not only by your intellect or knowledge of what God wants you to do but also by your desire and passion to accomplish it.

The Order

A seventh distinction is order. The order involves determining which comes first, the mission or the vision. To some extent this is the same question as *Which comes first, the chicken or the egg?* The point is that different people have different experiences and answer accordingly. Some have a vision of God's preferred future for their churches and later adopt a mission. Others begin with a mission and then develop a vision.

A vision is what the organization will look like as it realizes and accomplishes its mission in its ministry area. According to this definition, the organization must first know its mission. Then it moves on and considers its vision. The mission must exist before the vision or there will be no vision. From a logical and developmental perspective, the mission precedes the vision.

One way to develop a vision statement is to begin with the mission statement because it usually comes first. It's shorter and easier to develop first and then expand into the vision. This is a logical approach. First, you develop a mission statement. Next, you take the mission statement and ask, *What will this look like as we accomplish it in our ministry community?* If your ministry is a church, and its vision is the Great Commission, then what will your community look like as your church pursues, wins, and then disciples these people?

The Coherence

An eighth difference is coherence. In this context, coherence refers to how close together something is. It concerns unity, harmony, and agreement.

The missions of most ministry organizations are fairly common. Their mission statements will have more coherence than their vision statements. This is true in particular of the church. Those churches that follow Christ's directive have as their mission the Great Commission. While different churches will articulate the Commission in different ways, the essence is the same. If you were to make a list of fifteen or twenty biblical church mission statements, all would be slightly different. However, at the center of each would be the Great Commission mission.

The visions of most ministries, however, will be unique. Though the mission is common, the communities in which they are realized are not. Every community is different. The community may be inner-city, suburban, or rural. The ethnic makeup of the area may be predominantly Hispanic, African American, Asian, or Anglo. It may be affluent while another is poverty stricken. The community may consist of well-educated people while another consists of the uneducated. The vision filtered through a unique community will reflect these differences and will not be coherent from church to church.

The Focus

A ninth distinction is focus. The mission has a broad focus. Its purpose is to give the overview or the big picture. When people hear the mission, they have the broad umbrella that covers the ministry. If you were filming your church or parachurch ministry, the camera would back off and shoot from a distance in order to capture the mission.

The vision's focus is narrow. If you were filming your ministry's vision, the camera would move in close. A vision provides a picture of what Christ wants you to do. Pictures provide details. You look at a group shot of several people and you see distinctions such as different faces, clothes, and so on. Your vision will include such distinctions. If you are targeting an inner-city community, then you might see the poor and oppressed. If you have targeted a blue-collar community, then you will see people wearing blue jeans as opposed to a coat and tie.

The Effect

A tenth difference is effect. The effect refers to the result or consequence that the mission or vision has on people. The effect of the mission is to clarify for all what they are supposed to be doing. There are numerous trails that a ministry could take through the ministry maze. Some ministries, for example, are walking down the education trail. They see as their mission educated Christians—those who know their Bibles. Others are walking the evangelism trail. They exist to win souls. Still others are hiking across the social trail. They exist to help the disenfranchised and downcast. It is the mission that determines the organization's distinct ministry trail, and that determination is a mission's clarifying effect.

The effect of the vision isn't to clarify the organization's direction and function. To some extent it may do this; as people begin to see where they're going, some clarification will take place. However, the vision effect is to challenge. Once the leadership has clarified what they're supposed to be doing, the vision challenges them to do it. Both vision and mission are necessary. Knowing where you're going and getting there aren't the same. Your people may need some initial and long-term help in moving toward where they know they're supposed to be going. The vision serves this purpose. As people envision where the ministry can go, the vision challenges them to want to move and continue to move in that direction.

The Development

The eleventh distinction is development. In chapter 5 I covered the mission-development process. In chapter 8 I'll cover the vision-development process. The two processes, while having much in common, are unique. The development of a mission statement is more a science. Thus, it can be taught.

It's relatively easy to analyze and come up with some specific, concrete steps for mission development. I have found that these steps are relatively easy to teach to a board of leaders. And if they are unified in their core values, then you can come up with a mission statement in a few hours or a half day.

The development of the vision statement is more an art than a science. Thus, it's better caught than taught. I find in working with leaders that they have to *catch* the process. They catch on to the mission-development process faster than they catch on to the vision process. The result is that it takes much longer to develop the vision statement. It could happen over-night—though rare—but usually takes several months.

The Communication

The twelfth difference is how the two are communicated. The mission statement is best communicated visually—what is called the mission propagation process. While there are a variety of ways to communicate your mission, most are propagated visually. For example, you may place it on the front or back of a T-shirt. You may inscribe it on a wall plaque and place the plaque in high-visibility areas such as the church's foyer, along a well-traveled hall, and in certain rooms and offices. Many place it on the cover of the bulletin or a newsletter. Some have printed it on wallet-size cards, while others include it in a brochure or in a video. What do all these mediums have in common? They are perceived through the eyes.

You can also communicate your vision through visual means. While it will take up more room, you may be able to place it in a brochure or on a wall plaque. But that isn't the best, most effective way to communicate the vision. Visions are best communicated verbally, not visually. The power of the vision is in the hearing more than in the seeing. For example, the impact of Martin Luther King's vision statement as found in his sermon, "I Have a Dream," is greater when preached than when read off the printed page. To hear him preach this sermon with passion communicates better than simply reading it from a book.

	Mission	Vision
1. Definition	Statement	Snapshot
2. Application	Planning	Communication
3. Length	Short	Long
4. Purpose	Informs	Inspires
5. Activity	Doing	Seeing
6. Source	Head	Heart
7. Order	First	Second
8. Coherence	Common	Unique
9. Focus	Broad	Narrow
10. Effect	Clarifies	Challenges
11. Development	Science (taught)	Art (caught)
12. Communication	Visual	Verbal

Chart 7.1. The Differences Between a Mission and a Vision

QUESTIONS FOR REFLECTION, DISCUSSION, AND APPLICATION

The following questions assume that you either have a completed vision statement or that you have a good feel for what that vision will be. If you are at the front end of the vision-development process, you might want to answer these questions later.

1. Is your vision God's vision for your ministry? If no, why not? If yes, how do you know? Do you have any Scripture that supports your answer?

2. Is your vision future focused? Does it dwell in the past or focus on the future? Explain.

3. Is your vision direction-oriented? Do your people know where the ministry is going? If yes, why? If no, why not?

4. Is your vision function-oriented? Do your people know what they are supposed to be doing? If yes, what is it? If no, why not?

I have designed the following questions as a checklist to help you determine if your vision is truly a vision statement or a mission statement.

1. Is your vision a succinct statement of where the ministry is going or does it provide a picture of the same?

2. How do you plan to apply your vision statement to your church or parachurch ministry? Will you use it primarily for communication or planning?

3. How long is your vision statement? Is it longer than, the same size as, or shorter than your mission statement?

4. What is the purpose of your vision statement? Have you developed it primarily to inform or to inspire your people?

5. What kind of activity does your vision promote—doing or seeing?

6. What was the source of your vision? Did it come from what God put on your heart or in your head?

7. While it's not a final determiner of your vision, which came first, your vision or your mission?

8. At the core, does your vision have much in common with most other visions that you know of, or is it unique?

9. How focused is your vision? Is it very broad or is it detailed? Does it give you the big picture or does it provide many of the details?

10. What primary effect does your vision have on your people? Does it clarify for them where you're going and what you're supposed to be doing, or does it challenge them to go and to do?

11. In the development of your vision, was it more caught or taught? How long did it take you to develop it?
12. As a leader and communicator, what have you found to be the best way to communicate your vision to your followers—visually or verbally?

8

The Development of a Vision

How to Birth Your Vision

How do you birth a vision? What steps should a pastor and the board or others take to develop a clear challenging vision for a church? The answer is the three *p*s: the personnel, the process, and the product. The *personnel* are those who roll up their sleeves and do the actual vision work; the *process* will guide you through the steps for vision development; the section on *product* will provide you with several sample vision statements that are not only the result of the process but will also prove instructive.

VISION DEVELOPMENT PERSONNEL

The first issue to decide is who the ministry's vision developers will be. Who are the participants? Who are the personnel who will be directly involved in crafting a vision for the ministry's future? I asked this personnel question of the mission in chapter 5 and the values in chapter 2. A part of determining who's involved is to know your ministry's culture. For example, are your people blue or white collar? This is important because blue-collar people tend to look to their leaders to determine things such as their mission while white-collar people want to have some say in the process.

The Point Person

When it comes to the development of the vision, the process works differently. I believe that vision development is the primary responsibility of the point person on the ministry team because of leadership. The ability to craft and communicate a clear challenging vision is a key aspect of what it means to be a leader. Most would agree that vision is a significant quality of those who desire to lead a church or parachurch organization from the point position. This is because leaders must know where they're going. A nonvisionary can accomplish this to some degree, but he or she naturally tends to focus on the present and what is. To focus on the future is more difficult, less natural, and takes more effort. A visionary intuitively focuses on the future and what could be. For visionaries, this takes place naturally and with little thought to the process.

The importance of being a visionary to leadership and vision development raises the question, *How can you know if you're a visionary?* There are several ways to find out. One is to take the Myers-Briggs Type Indicator (MBTI) test.[1] It seeks to determine if you are a sensing or an intuitive type person. The sensing type is the nonvisionary practical realist while the intuitive type is the visionary. Another approach is to take the Kiersey-Bates Temperament Sorter. It's much shorter than the Myers-Briggs and easier to obtain. You can find it along with a complete explanation in the book *Please Understand Me*.[2] A third way is to take the inventory in appendix F in this book. Though it's very short and not as accurate as the two tools above, it may give you a read on your visionary or realist preference.

What if you're the leader of a ministry but you're not a visionary? This is a question that people have frequently asked me. In an ideal world, I believe that the senior pastor of a church and the primary leader of a parachurch ministry should be a visionary. As stated above, vision is a vital aspect of leadership. In the real world, though, such often isn't the case. It may be one reason why so many churches in America remain small. (Though most people attend large churches, most churches are small.) What should you do if you are a nonvisionary in a primary leadership position? The answer is to stay where you are, but if your ministry is to move into the future, you'll have to come up with some ways to cast vision. You might discover, however, that you're more comfortable in a less visionary role such as that of a support pastor. Should this be your situation, then slowly transition yourself to such a position, preferably in another ministry.

The Ministry Team

If the cultivation of the vision is the primary responsibility of the point person, what is the role of the others on the ministry team? How will they gain ownership of the vision if they're not significantly involved?

Though the leader is responsible to see that vision development happens, that doesn't necessarily mean he or she is tasked with the entire development of the organization's vision. In some situations, this may be the case. However, I would want to heavily involve my ministry-team people. When I consult with churches on vision development, I make sure that twenty to twenty-five of the church's core leaders—the Strategic Leadership Team—are a vital part of the process. I would do the same as a pastor. The reason is that fewer people—especially today's younger people—trust something that comes completely and totally from the pastor alone. Also, you want the team itself to own the vision. This won't happen unless they're involved in the process.

VISION DEVELOPMENT PROCESS

Now that you know who the primary vision people are, the next question is, *How do these people team up to craft the vision? What process should you follow?* First, you must prepare yourself to develop the vision. Then you have at least three options for how you'll develop your ministry's vision statement.

Preparation for Vision Development

You'll need to take several steps to prepare yourself to develop a God-honoring vision.

Pray. The first step is prayer. While all prayer is vital to this process, envisioning prayer is essential. An example of such a prayer is found in Nehemiah 1. Ask God to give you a specific picture of what his vision is for your ministry. Then don't forget about it—start the process of expectant looking. Don't be surprised when ideas, pictures, and thoughts begin to pop into your head.

Think Big. I find that too many people who are, or want to be, leaders think small. This problem is prevalent among seminarians. I suspect it's because so much of their training in school forces them to think analytically and not synthetically. They get the details but miss the big picture. Jesus didn't think small. In Mark 16:15 he says, "Go into all the world and preach the good news to all creation." That's thinking big. Paul, in Ephesians 3:20, appears to give the church at Ephesus a slap on the wrist for not asking and thinking big enough: "Now to him who is able to do immeasurably more than all we ask or imagine, according to his power that is at work within us . . ." How big are your prayers? How big is your vision? Do you pray and think big enough?

Brainstorm Verbally and in Writing. As you think and pray big about your vision, consider writing down what God brings to mind. The process of brainstorming teaches you to consider all thoughts that come to mind. Verbalize these thoughts and write them down so that you don't lose them. Reserve any evaluation or judgment until later. The act of verbalizing aids the memory process, and the act of writing them down blows any mental dust or cobwebs off your brain. Writing sharpens your thinking.

Question the Dream. As your vision takes shape in your mind or on paper, probe it with questions. Use the definition of vision—a clear, challenging picture of the future of the ministry as you believe it can and must be—as a test for your vision. Do the self-test and the people test.

- Is it clear? Do I understand it? Do others understand it?
- Does it challenge me? Does it challenge others?
- Does it create a picture in my mind? Can others see where we're going?
- Is it futuristic? Does it serve as a bridge that will take us from our present to our preferred future? When our people hear it, does it focus their thoughts on the future?
- Do you believe that this vision is even possible? Should you quit now before you make a fool of yourself and a laughingstock of the ministry? Or do you find yourself stretched by the reality of what God is putting on your heart?
- Are you convinced that this vision must be? Do you feel strongly about it? Do others?

If your answers or others' answers to any of these questions are negative, then go back to work. Keep at it until the answers are positive. Ask others what it would take for the vision or some aspect of it to get a positive answer.

Demonstrate Patience. I have already warned you that it may take longer to develop the vision than to develop the mission. Take whatever time is necessary to get it done. It may come quickly; it may take some time.

Now that you know how to prepare to develop your vision, you next need to decide which of three approaches you might take: expand the mission statement, build on your core values, or model after another vision statement.

Expand the Mission Statement

A good way to develop a powerful, challenging vision is to expand the mission statement. This assumes that you have followed the order in this book (values, mission, vision, and strategy) and have developed the mission statement first. Start with the completed mission statement. Then ask, *What will the ministry look like as it accomplishes this mission in its ministry context or community?*

When working with a strategic leadership team, I sometimes use the following approach. I divide them into groups of two to four people. I give them a copy of their mission statement or write it on a whiteboard where all can see it. I also ask them to choose a recorder, and I give that person one or two four-by-six-inch cards. Then I ask them to describe what it will look like when their church begins to realize its mission. The recorder is responsible to record the results, and I ask this person to read to the entire group what his or her small group came up with. When finished, they pass these cards to the pastor or leader of the team. If the pastor is a strong, creative visionary, he serves as the final editor of the vision statement so that he has his visionary fingerprints all over the final product.

Build on the Core Values

A second approach to vision development is to build off your core values that you discovered and articulated earlier. Here is an example that was developed by one of my students, Paul Srch, for church planting. The first statement is his articulation of one of his core values followed by a vision for that value:

Value: A Commitment to Creative Evangelism

Unchurched people matter to God and thus must matter to us as well. Therefore, we will provide opportunities for them to hear the good news of Jesus Christ in creative ways through a variety of means and media so that they respond in faith.

But what does this look like? What will people see when the church begins to put this value into action—to live it out in its ministry community? The answer is the following vision:

We see friends bringing friends to a Sunday morning seeker-focused service because they will hear the good news presented clearly and creatively in an atmosphere of acceptance. . . .

We dream of a church communicating the message of Christ to lost people, using multimedia, the arts, and the Internet. . . .

We hear believers sharing their faith at work over coffee, at home around the dinner table, at the park while their kids are playing. . . .

We see new believers being baptized as a testimony to lives changed by God's grace. . . .

We envision forming a network of healthy churches that in turn plant other churches, throughout McHenry County and beyond!

In presenting these to your congregation, you could either combine the values credo with the vision statement, or you could separate them into different documents.

When working with a strategic leadership team, I follow a similar process to that of expanding the mission statement. However, I will assign each two- to four-person team one value and ask them to expand it into a vision statement.

Model After Another Vision

A third approach is to model your vision after another's vision. I suspect that when most of us read or hear various vision statements, we have our favorites. Some click with us. They ignite our passion, while others do not. We might even wonder why a particular leader has chosen and developed it. Nonetheless, God is using it with different leaders and people in a different context.

This approach would challenge you to find one that grabs your attention. When you hear or see it, you take a second look. It moves you deeply and inspires you. Then you would use it as a pattern or working model to develop your own. You would not necessarily even use the same words. Regardless, it serves to get you started in the process, and you launch from there.

When working with a strategic leadership team, I give each two- to four-person team a copy of the vision statement. I ask them to discuss the statement in light of what they see two, five, ten, even twenty years from now and write their responses on the copy. After sharing some of their ideas with the entire team, the leader collects the copies, edits, and collates the group's work into the final vision product.

VISION DEVELOPMENT PRODUCT

The fruit of the visionary's labor is the vision. Studying other people's vision statements can be as instructive as working through the development process yourself. One of my friends refers to this process as a "vision dump." That's an unfortunate term perhaps, as these examples merely serve for the sake of vision clarity—to give the visionary leader several samples of what a good vision looks like. You can learn much from seeing what others have included or excluded from their statements. There is the danger, however, of adopting someone else's vision statement that doesn't fit you or your church or parachurch organization. That's why it's important for you to walk through the process first.

In this section, I present several excellent vision statements with a brief examination and explanation of each. They are all vision sermons or talks. While I have written these down, their power is not only in how they read but also in how the speaker says them. We lose that effect in a study like this.

God's Vision Statement for Israel

The first is God's vision for his people as communicated through Moses. This becomes Moses' vision statement for Israel. In chapter 4, I presented Moses' mission statement: "So now, go. I am sending you to Pharaoh to bring my people the Israelites out of Egypt" (Exod. 3:10). This mission is expanded in God's vision for his people: "So I have come down to rescue them from the hand of the Egyptians and to bring them up out of that land into a good and spacious land, a land flowing with milk and honey—the home of the Canaanites, Hittites, Amorites, Perizzites, Hivites and Jebusites" (Exod. 3:8). Moses will cast and recast this vision in a number of places as recorded throughout the Pentateuch (Exod. 13:5; Deut. 8:7–9; 11:9). Noteworthy is Deuteronomy 8:7–9:

> For the LORD your God is bringing you into a good land—a land
> with streams and pools of water, with springs flowing in the val-
> leys and hills; a land with wheat and barley, vines and fig trees,
> pomegranates, olive oil and honey; a land where bread will not be
> scarce and you will lack nothing; a land where the rocks are iron
> and you can dig copper out of the hills.

Moses simply expands the mission statement. He creates a vivid picture of what their future life will look like and be like in the Promised Land. You can enter somewhat into the experience of the Israelite as you hear this vision. You can't help seeing streams and pools of water, wheat and barley waving in the breeze, trees with luscious figs and ripe pomegranates. You can almost taste the honey and feel its stickiness between your fingers. You can smell the fresh bread baking in the oven.

Martin Luther King Jr.'s Vision for America

Another vision statement, and one of the most famous in recent American history, is the vision of Martin Luther King Jr. While it depicts what he saw when he envisioned the future of African Americans in this country, it also pictures what he saw when he envisioned every American's future. It's his vision for America:

> I say to you today, my friends, that in spite of the difficulties
> and frustrations of the moment I still have a dream. It is a dream
> deeply rooted in the American dream.
>
> I have a dream that one day this nation will rise up and live out
> the true meaning of its creed: "We hold these truths to be self-
> evident; that all men are created equal."
>
> I have a dream that one day on the red hills of Georgia the sons
> of former slaves and the sons of former slave owners will be able to
> sit down together at the table of brotherhood.

I have a dream that one day even the state of Mississippi, a desert state sweltering with the heat of injustice and oppression, will be transformed into an oasis of freedom and justice.

I have a dream that my four little children will one day live in a nation where they will be judged not by the color of their skin but by the content of their character.

I have a dream today. I have a dream that one day the state of Alabama, whose governor's lips are presently dripping with the words of interposition and nullification, will be transformed into a situation where little black boys and black girls will be able to join hands with little white boys and white girls and walk together as sisters and brothers.

I have a dream today. I have a dream that one day every valley shall be exalted, every hill and mountain shall be made low, the rough places will be made plains, and the crooked places will be made straight, and the glory of the Lord shall be revealed, and all flesh shall see it together.

This is our hope. This is the faith with which I return to the South. With this faith we will be able to transform the jangling discords of our nation into a beautiful symphony of brotherhood. With this faith we will be able to work together, to pray together, to struggle together, to go to jail together, to stand up for freedom together, knowing that we will be free one day.

This will be the day when all God's children will be able to sing with new meaning, "My country 'tis of thee, sweet land of liberty, of thee I sing. Land where my fathers died, land of the pilgrim's pride, from every mountainside, let freedom ring."

And if America is to be a great nation this must become true. So let freedom ring from the prodigious hilltops of New Hampshire. Let freedom ring from the mighty mountains of New York. Let freedom ring from the heightening Alleghenies of Pennsylvania!

Let freedom ring from the snowcapped Rockies of Colorado! Let freedom ring from the curvaceous peaks of California! But not only that; let freedom ring from the Stone Mountain of Georgia! Let freedom ring from every hill and molehill of Mississippi. From every mountainside, let freedom ring.

When we let freedom ring, when we let it ring from every village and every hamlet, from every state and every city, we will be able to speed up that day when all of God's children, black men and white men, Jews and Gentiles, Protestants and Catholics, will be able to join hands and sing in the words of that old Negro spiritual, "Free at last! Free at last! Thank God almighty, we are free at last!"[3]

You will find the key to this vision statement in the second paragraph. It's all about freedom and liberty. It concerns the fundamental truth that God has created all men, including black people in America, equal. He could have said all of this in one, or at the most, two paragraphs. But that isn't how visions work. He expands his message, describing what equality, freedom, and justice would look like in America. Statements such as "the sons of former slaves and the sons of former slave owners will sit down together at the table of brotherhood" and "little black boys and black girls will be able to join hands with little white boys and white girls" are picturesque. You can't help seeing what he's talking about. You see black people and white people sitting together at a table. You see little black children and white children holding hands. The reason? That's what freedom looks like.

The lesson for the visionary is to pin down a central idea or theme (this is good homiletics). For Martin Luther King Jr., it was freedom. For you it might be a great church. Then describe in words what you see in your head when you dream about that central idea. What does freedom look like? What does a great church look like? What do you see when you think about freedom or a great church? The question to constantly address is, *What do you see?*

Pastors' Vision for Lakeview Community Church

Lakeview Community Church is a recently planted church in Cedar Hill, Texas, a town located south of the Dallas-Fort Worth Metroplex. The founding pastor and assistant pastor developed the following vision statement:

> This statement lays the philosophical foundation for the establishment and continuing ministry of the Lakeview Community Church of Cedar Hill, Texas. It represents our understanding of the unique role God has called us to fulfill in the world, as expressed in our purpose and our principles. We believe that by clearly identifying these things, we will be better equipped to accomplish the task God has given us.
>
> Our comprehensive purpose is to honor our Lord and Savior, Jesus Christ, by carrying out his command to make disciples of all nations (Matt. 28:18–20). Specifically, we believe God has called us to focus on reaching those in Cedar Hill and the surrounding areas who do not regularly attend any church. In order to accomplish this, Lakeview Community Church will be an equipping center where every Christian can be developed to his or her potential for ministry. This development will come through
>
> a) creative, inspiring worship.
>
> b) teaching which is Biblical and relevant to life.
>
> c) vital, supportive fellowship.
>
> d) opportunities for outreach into the community in service and evangelism.
>
> As a result, the Cedar Hill area will be different in ten to fifteen years, with the Christian influence being increasingly felt in homes, businesses, education, and politics. We further intend to multiply our world-wide ministry by planting churches, by preparing our people for leadership roles in vocational ministries and parachurch groups, by sending out missionaries, and by becoming a resource center and model for Texas and the nation.

After an introductory paragraph to orient the reader to the vision statement, the drafters discuss several areas in detail. First, they provide the mission or purpose of the church—to make disciples of all nations. (The remaining areas are an expansion of this mission or purpose.) Second, they identify their target group—unchurched people in Cedar Hill and the surrounding areas. Next, the writers identify the church as a center to equip its people to do ministry. They follow this with a four-point strategy that explains how they will equip the church. Finally, they describe the impact that the church will have not only on the Cedar Hill area but also on the state of Texas and the world.

Pictures should begin to surface as they talk about reaching "those in Cedar Hill and the surrounding areas who do not regularly attend church." Perhaps the most graphic is the last paragraph where they focus on such things as homes, businesses, education, politics, church planting, and the sending out of missionaries.

This vision is also an excellent example of thinking big. The idea at the end of sending out missionaries and "becoming a resource center and model for Texas and the nation" takes Ephesians 3:20 and the Great Commission seriously.

Rick Warren's Vision for Saddleback Valley Community Church

Pastor Rick Warren planted Saddleback Community Church in 1980. It's located in Mission Viejo, California, south of Los Angeles. He cast the following vision for the church in a sermon that he delivered on March 30, 1980:

> **It is the dream** of a place where the hurting, the depressed, the frustrated, and the confused can find love, acceptance, help, hope, forgiveness, guidance, and encouragement.
>
> **It is the dream** of sharing the Good News of Jesus Christ with the hundreds of thousands of residents in south Orange County.
>
> **It is the dream** of welcoming 20,000 members into the fellowship of our church family—loving, learning, laughing, and living in harmony together.

It is the dream of developing people to spiritual maturity through Bible studies, small groups, seminars, retreats, and a Bible school for our members.

It is the dream of equipping every believer for a significant ministry by helping them discover the gifts and talents God gave them.

It is the dream of sending out hundreds of career missionaries and church workers all around the world, and empowering every member for a personal life mission in the world. It is the dream of sending our members by the thousands on short-term mission projects to every continent. It is the dream of starting at least one new daughter church every year.

It is the dream of at least fifty acres of land, on which will be built a regional church for south Orange County—with beautiful, yet simple, facilities including a worship center seating thousands, a counseling and prayer center, classrooms for Bible studies and training lay ministers, and a recreation area. All of this will be designed to minister to the total person—spiritually, emotionally, physically, and socially—and set in a peaceful inspiring garden landscape.

I stand before you today and state in confident assurance that these dreams will become reality. Why? Because they are inspired by God![4]

Pastor Rick Warren has taken a topical approach to vision development. Each paragraph presents his dream on a particular topic affecting the future of the church. There are seven topics. The first is his vision for people—the hurting, depressed, and so on. The second topic is evangelism—"sharing the Good News of Jesus Christ." The third is members of the church family. Note that here he sets a numerical goal of twenty thousand members. The fourth topic is his dream for his church's spiritual maturity accompanied by a strategy. The fifth topic is lay involvement or empowerment—it is his vision to equip all of his people for ministry. The sixth is missions—the sending out of lay and career missionaries all over the world. The final topic is land and facilities that will contribute to the development of the total person. Note that the second through sixth topics are vital parts of the Saddleback strategy.

As a visionary, Rick Warren took these various topics and dreamed about them. As in this case, when pictures came to mind he both preached them and wrote them down. Essentially, Rick expanded each topic into a full-blown picture of what the church would look like in the future. He may have done this by design, or it may have simply come to mind, as happens with visionaries.

Tim Armstrong's Vision for Crossroads Community Church

Tim Armstrong is a graduate of Dallas Seminary. During his last year of seminary, he initiated the planting of Crossroads Community Church near Mansfield, Ohio. The following is his vision for this church:

> The writer of Proverbs wrote, "Where there is no vision the people perish" (29:18 KJV). At Crossroads, it is our desire that you catch the vision God has given us, that you begin to visualize the invisible! We have worked hard at defining our vision so that it is clear, challenging, and concise. It is our desire that you clearly see the future of the ministry—what it can be and what it must be. But most importantly, we want you to capture the concept of our vision so that it will capture you and provide a foundation for your personal ministry with us at Crossroads.
>
> In part, the vision of Crossroads Community Church is to become a biblically functioning community. This will become clear as you continue through the notebook. However, our complete vision statement more specifically defines our desires.

Crossroads Vision Statement

The vision of Crossroads Community Church is to creatively implement the Great Commission to build a growing community of churches around the perimeter of Mansfield by planting culturally relevant churches every three years that are committed to dynamic worship of God while extending His transforming grace to reach the unchurched community.

There are five key phrases that outline our vision. They represent the core of our vision and are essential for evaluating, redefining, and sharpening our focus. The five key phrases are

"Creatively Implement the Great Commission"

Jesus summarized his purpose for being on earth in Luke 19:10. He said, "For the Son of Man came to seek and to save that which was lost" (KJV). In his final instructions he made the purposes of the church clear. "Go and make disciples of all nations, baptizing them in the name of the Father and of the Son and of the Holy Spirit, and teaching them to obey everything I have commanded you" (Matt. 28:19–20). Therefore, our vision includes pursuing the lost in the most culturally relevant format. This includes implementing Christ's commission in both an innovative and creative manner to the unchurched people of our community.

"Build a Growing Community of Churches"

Unchurched people are nine times more likely to come to a new church rather than an older, established church (*Christianity Today*). We feel that the best means of impacting our area with the transforming message of Christ is to plant culturally relevant churches, like Crossroads, around our community. For us, this means starting a new church every three years in strategic locations so as to build a perimeter of churches around the city.

"Committed to Dynamic Worship"

Because our vision is to extend the transforming grace of Jesus Christ, we believe that the most fundamental relationship people can have is an active, living relationship with God through Jesus Christ His Son (John 10:10; Rom. 6:23). Our worship services reflect this by promoting creative, inspiring and authentic worship which demonstrates that God is living and active in this generation; therefore, the most contemporary medium is used to express our worship.

"Extending His Transforming Grace"

By the grace of God, the city of Ontario will be a changed community in ten to fifteen years, due to the influence of the Spirit of God through the lives of our people who are devoted to extending the transforming grace of Jesus Christ. It is our vision that the members of Crossroads will take Christ into homes, marketplaces, political arenas, and educational settings. Our Sunday morning service reflects our vision by being a safe place for Crossroads members to bring their friends, relatives, and coworkers. In other words, Crossroads is a safe place to hear a dangerous message.

"Reach the Unchurched"

Finally, our vision includes the intentional pursuit of reaching those who have stopped attending, or have never attended a church. In other words, those who have not experienced God's transforming grace.

Placing a vision in print is somewhat like attempting to hold water in your hand. It is nearly impossible! A vision is something that is caught rather than taught. Vision has been described as a mental picture of the future that finds its realization in the hands of the one who owns the vision. It is our desire that the Crossroads vision becomes your vision; something you "own" and take great pride in seeing fulfilled. In essence, our vision is not something that you can see, but something you must be.

After a two-paragraph introduction, Pastor Tim Armstrong presents a full, one sentence vision statement. It consists of a "what" and a "how." The *what* is to implement the Great Commission around the perimeter of Mansfield, Ohio. The *how* is to plant churches, and the first is Crossroads Community Church of Ontario, Ohio. Then he lifts "five key phrases" out of the statement and expands each.

You should note the practice of expanding in vision drafting. Earlier I stated that the best way to craft a ministry vision is to begin with a mission statement. Once you've developed the mission, then you develop your vision by expanding that mission statement. This has proved true of all the vision statements above. Here, Pastor Tim begins with a statement that some would say is his mission statement. I would describe it as a mini*vision* statement because it consists of his mission (the what) and strategy (the how). Regardless, it contains the essential ingredients of his vision. All that remains is for him to dream and picture what each of these ingredients will look like as the church realizes its mission and strategy. In this vision statement, he has chosen to write down, for his people and potential members, what he sees.

Bill Hybels's Vision for Willow Creek Community Church

Bill Hybels is the senior pastor of Willow Creek Community Church, which is located in Barrington, Illinois, just west of Chicago. On numerous occasions over the thirty-plus-year history of Willow Creek, Hybels has cast and recast his vision for the church. An example is "Vision Night '96." This vision event was very strategic in the life of the church because it marked their twenty-year anniversary and set the course of the church for the next five years.

It's not feasible to include Hybels's sermon here. In summary, he crafted the entire sermon around the church's strategic plan for the next five years. In this sermon, he conveys the plan and describes what he sees as he pictures Willow Creek's future in the Chicago area. The vision talk communicates three major goals or what Hybels calls three "big ideas" or "values." The first goal is, "We feel we need to reach an ever-increasing percentage of the Chicago-land area with the gospel message." The second is, "We are going to move the congregation of Christ followers toward community, spiritual maturity, and full participation in the life of the church." And the last goal is, "We are going to invest a greater percentage of our lives and our knowledge and our resources with those in our city, our nation, and our world."

Next, he elaborates on the strategy or how the church plans to accomplish each of these big ideas. Many of them affect their programs. For example, the church will implement the first evangelistic goal by training members in evangelism, inviting seekers to a weekend service and to the small-group meetings, conducting outreach concerts, and helping other churches in the community to become evangelistically intense.

Third, Hybels announces that the ministry team at Willow Creek has set a numerical figure for each major goal. The figure for the first is to have more than twenty thousand people in attendance at the weekend services. The figure for the second is eight thousand people at the New Community service, and the third is eight thousand people serving in ministries outside Willow Creek. This is a great example of the importance of thinking big as Paul encourages in Ephesians 3:20.

Fourth, someone on the leadership team has taken responsibility for each major goal. For example, Lee Strobel has volunteered to become the point person for the first goal, John Ortburg the second goal, and John Burke the third. They will function as the point person to gather the other leaders around them to make sure that the entire staff and all the leaders of the church are working together toward this goal.

Finally, it's important to vision development and casting to note how Hybels (as well as the others) says what he says. His use of words, phrases, and statements is powerful. He describes the goal of evangelizing Chicago as "an all-out full-court press." He is counting on the witness of the church "to burn brightly." He speaks of taking risks as "being free with and even reckless with" the gospel. He talks about "evangelistic intensity." He describes the initiation of the program as "the starting gun goes off and we charge into the future." He hopes that his people will be "contagious Christians." And he's going "to turn up the thermostat at the weekend services."

Andy McQuithy's Vision for Irving Bible Church

Pastor Andy McQuithy has done a masterful job at leading Irving Bible Church through a re-envisioning process that has resulted in the revitalization of the church.

Our Dreams

About 10 years ago we developed a series of statements of what we dreamed IBC would become. The statements that follow have withstood the test of time and still reflect the heart of what is going on with IBC.

We dream of a church . . .

. . . where the Gospel is the underlying theme; where grace is accepted and extended; where the salvation of souls is the norm, not the exception; where love for people springs from love for God; where joy permeates the air; where people are one in spirit; where service is considered a privilege not a burden.

. . . where people find real help, experience real change and discover real answers; where marriages are healed and parents' hearts are turned toward their children; where destructive lifestyles, habits, addictions, and compulsions are forever jettisoned; where wasted lives are retrieved and new beginnings launched.

. . . where God's Word is exalted in authority, studied with expectation, taught with relevance, heard with anticipation, and obeyed with passion; where the preaching is encouraging, positive, and practical.

. . . where prayer is the under-girding and engulfing medium for all we do and for every initiative we take.

. . . where people are free to attempt great things for God; where taking risks for his kingdom is an exalted virtue; where people have nothing to prove and therefore nothing to lose; where creativity and innovation are honored, not feared; where all kinds of people serve God in diverse ways with mutual love, encouragement, respect, and unity.

. . . where people's hearts beat for God's work around the world; where impact is made on lives across the street and around the world; where short-term workers regularly go out to minister internationally and return with a world perspective.

. . . where the challenge of nurturing new, cutting-edge ministries becomes reality; where past traditions form the foundations for launching new innovations, not the ball and chain to impede them; where hundreds of lay men and women are effectively trained and actually entrusted with the work of the ministry; where partnerships are formed by networking with other ministries to further the cause of Christ.

. . . where children and youth are nurtured in the faith; where they are made strong in their ability to serve the Lord and stand for him in their world.

. . . where God is worshiped joyfully and reverently; where the music is Christ-honoring and relevant; where worship is a significant event that encourages believers and transforms them into the triumphant army of God; where worship communicates to the visitor the greatness of our God, the joyfulness of the Christian life, and the emptiness of life without Jesus.

. . . where the issues of our culture are seriously addressed; where the community expects to find a viewpoint both practical and godly, a viewpoint that must be taken seriously; where God's courageous and compassionate people take stands in the community.

. . . where growth is not only welcomed, but anticipated as the norm; where the heartbeat of every person is for outreach and inclusion, not for comfortable complacency and seclusion.

QUESTIONS FOR REFLECTION, DISCUSSION, AND APPLICATION

1. Will the development of the vision be the primary domain of the ministry leader? Who will be the personnel involved in the drafting of your ministry's vision? Are these people visionaries or practical realists? How do you know? Have they taken the Myers-Briggs Type Indicator or the Kiersey-Bates Temperament Sorter? Why or why not?

2. How will the other significant people in the ministry contribute to

the crafting of the vision? How might the practical realists contribute? How might the other visionaries help?

3. Have you developed the mission before attempting to draft the vision? Why or why not? Have you skipped over the first two parts of this book because someone has convinced you that your primary ministry need is a powerful, significant vision? How will parts 1 and 2 of this book be beneficial to the crafting of a vision?

4. How much time do you have, or plan to spend, to pray for your vision? Is it or will it be big enough? How do you know? Are you at least verbalizing if not writing down your thoughts as you work through the envisioning process?

5. Is your vision clear? Challenging? Does it prompt pictures in people's minds? Does it focus on the future? Do you believe that your vision is possible? Do you have a passion to see it through to its realization?

6. Why is it important that you go through the envisioning process before adopting a vision? What's wrong, if anything, with using another ministry's vision? Is it okay to put together different parts from other statements to form your own, unique vision?

7. In this chapter, I have presented several vision statements. Which did you like best? What was it that attracted you to it? Which didn't you care for? Why?

8. How will these statements help you in developing your vision? Could you use some or all of them in some way to communicate your vision at various times and at various events in the life of your ministry? Does their use of language help or inspire you in some way?

Part 4

The Strategy for Your Ministry

9

The Definition of Strategy

What Is a Strategy?

Now that you have a clear direction, consisting of a ministry mission and vision, it's imperative that the ministry team rethink and develop a clear, high-impact strategy to implement that direction in general and the mission in particular. The strategy is the vehicle that enables the church to bring about its mission. It accomplishes little if the trailer shows up without its tractor. The strategy also helps your people to understand why they're doing what they're doing. Far too many people are going through the motions without understanding. The strategy explains why they attend a worship service, a small group, or a special seminar as well as other events. Finally, a strategy provides a sense of momentum or progress. A good strategy takes its people through the discipleship-development process. This process has clear, discernible steps. As people take those steps, they gain a sense of spiritual momentum—they are going somewhere spiritually. On the one hand, it's encouraging for them to look back and see where they've been. On the other hand, it's challenging for them to see where they have yet to go.

Before the leader and his team begin to develop their mission strategy, they need to make sure that they understand what a strategy is. It can prove embarrassing to attempt something only to discover you didn't fully understand what you were attempting: the leader orders his followers, "Charge the hill!" and some people pull out their credit cards while others load their guns. How many times have we differed with someone over an issue, only to understand later that we weren't even talking about the same thing? Clear communication is the key. What, then, is a strategy? What is *not* a strategy? What kinds of strategies are there? And what are the five elements that make up an effective strategy?

WHAT A STRATEGY IS NOT

As with the other concepts of this book, I believe that you will best understand the mission strategy if I define what it isn't as well as what it is. Leaders may confuse the strategy with a number of other concepts such as values, mission, and vision. I see this confusion in discussions of these concepts in the marketplace, though a strategy is most commonly confused with a plan.

Although an organizational strategy is commonly equated with an organizational plan, they're not the same. They are often used as synonyms, and the two do have some similarities. Both, for example, answer the *how* question: How will we charge the hill? How will we accomplish our ministry mission?

Their differences, however, far exceed their commonalties. The strategy is a part of the plan but not the same as the plan. The plan is much broader and subsumes the strategy along with a number of other concepts. A plan *is* one of the ministry ABCs. However, I have chosen not to cover ministry planning as it's too vast a concept for this book, and a number of books are already available on the topic.[1] The important point is that you see the difference between the strategy and the plan, and that you realize that your work isn't complete once you've developed your strategy. Strategy must fit within the context of a ministry plan.

A second distinction is orientation. The strategy is action oriented, not intention oriented. A plan is exactly that—a plan for action. Whereas a strategy *is* the action. In a plan, leaders and administrators set forth their ministry goals and objectives. In a strategy, they attempt to accomplish those goals and objectives. Leaders tend to drift toward strategizing; administrators tend to favor planning. A person with the gift of leadership and administration is strong as a primary leader because he or she favors both.

In *Managing the Non-Profit Organization*, Peter Drucker illustrates the distinction: "Good intentions don't move mountains, bulldozers do."[2] Strategies are bulldozers—they're action oriented. Plans are good intentions—they're intention oriented. Drucker states that planning is what you want to do—an intellectual exercise, good intentions. Strategy is your accomplishments. Strategy transforms intentions into actions. It involves not wanting to do something but doing it. In planning, we say that we intend to "take the hill," in strategizing, we "take the hill."

On the surface, these distinctions may seem minor and, indeed, the literature on the subject uses both terms casually and almost interchangeably. You, however, must be careful in the use of the terms *strategy* and *plan*, or reap confusion.

WHAT A STRATEGY IS

A strategy is the process that determines how you will accomplish the mission as well as the vision of your ministry. This definition has three vital concepts.

A Strategy Has a Mission

First, a strategy must have a mission. According to chapter 4 every ministry must have a mission and should articulate that mission in a mission statement. The crying need in many if not most churches in North America is for them to know where they're going. As one church elder and chairman of the board recently said to me, "We desperately need some direction!"

A church without a mission is like a plane without a destination. I frequently fly out of Love Field in Dallas, Texas. It has many advantages over the huge Dallas–Fort Worth Airport located equidistant between Dallas and Fort Worth. Two of those advantages are proximity to Dallas and ease of parking. I also like to fly Southwest Airlines, which only flies out of Love Field. Southwest is a customer-friendly airline. When you board the plane, for example, often the captain is standing at the door to greet you. I enjoy joking with the pilots. But can you imagine my consternation if I asked the pilot, jokingly, "Where are we going?" and he or she soberly responded, "Beats me, I don't have a clue!" Yet many of our churches, when asked where they're going, soberly respond, "We don't have a clue!" Would you climb on board?

What is amazing to me is that all of these churches have a strategy. A church has to have ministries to keep its doors open. They have to have something in place for people to come to. The ministries are the end product of a strategy. If you examine a church's ministries, you will learn much about its strategy. Most older, traditional churches for years have followed the three-to-thrive programming concept. They meet Sunday morning for Sunday school and a preaching and worship service. They meet Sunday night for a preaching service. Finally, they meet Wednesday night for prayer. These programs reflect a strategy. The strategy is to teach people God's Word, to worship, and to pray.

If you ask these churches why they are doing these important things, however, they blink and become quiet. Some will respond with, "We've always done it that way!" This is true, but it is hardly an adequate answer. What has happened is the church over the years has lost sight of its mission. When it was founded, the mission was clear. The core group and the planting pastor knew what they were supposed to be doing. They also developed the three-to-thrive strategy to accomplish the mission. Along with the strategy, they implemented the various programs that reflect that strategy.

Over time, the founding pastor left and was followed by other pastors. In the exchange of the pastoral baton, somehow the church misplaced the mission while the programs became hardened tradition. It's tragic that not only did they lose the mission, but the programs reflect America as it was in the 1930s, 1940s, and 1950s. What is wrong with that? We no longer live in that time. People have changed and the country has changed. The culture is no longer church friendly. And Christ's church must change and target America's lost and dying unchurched population. They are the future not only of this country, they are also the future of the church.

Strategy begins by taking part 2 of this book seriously and developing a dynamic, biblical mission. We must determine what God's mission is for our ministries. We must discover what it is that God wants us to do. Pastors and leaders must ask and answer the question, *Where is this plane going after it leaves the airport?* Once they have a biblical answer, then they must pursue it with a passion. Key to that pursuit is a strategy that is both relevant to and understanding of today's world and the world of tomorrow.

A Strategy Is a Process

A strategy isn't static, it involves a process. It's the process of moving people from prebirth to maturity. Prebirth refers to that period in one's life when he or she is not a Christian. I have labeled it prebirth because it takes place before the new birth (John 3:1–7). The prebirth stage begins at physical birth and lasts up to the new birth. You will find non-Christians at various stages of unbelief during the prebirth period. Some may be far from the Savior, such as Herod (Acts 12:21–23) and Saul (Acts 8:1–3). Others may be seekers and very close to faith as were Nicodemus (John 3), Zacchaeus (Luke 19:3), the Ethiopian eunuch (Acts 8:26), and Cornelius (Acts 10).

The maturity stage begins at new birth (conversion) and lasts until the Christian dies and joins his or her Savior. I use the word *maturity* optimistically. It describes what should happen during this time. The process is for believers to move from new birth to maturity or Christlikeness (Col. 1:28–29; 2:6–7).

According to research done for the Evangelical Free Church of America by Bob Gilliam, this process isn't happening in our churches. He conducted a survey that included four thousand attendees in thirty-five churches in several denominations from Florida to Washington. Gilliam discovered the following:

- There is absolutely no correlation between the length of time a person had been a Christian and their level of maturity.
- Many persons do not understand the meaning of discipleship or the spiritual disciplines. For instance, it is very common for people to report that they did have a regular daily quiet time with God, but in a later question state that they only did this about twice a year.
- Most people in these churches are not growing spiritually. Of those taking the survey, 24 percent indicated that their behavior was sliding backward and 41 percent said they were "static" in their spiritual growth.[3]

The strategy process recognizes that people are at different places in their spiritual journeys. Scripture acknowledges this as well (Matt. 13:18–23). You design the process to move people from wherever they are spiritually (lost or saved) to where God wants them to be (spiritually mature). Therefore, a person in your church or a new person to your ministry will find that the strategy is tailor-made for him or her. A program is in place for each person.

Numerous ways are available to communicate the process. One is Engel's Scale (see fig. 9.1).[4] This scale is a continuum that represents the process of moving a lost person from one extreme (no knowledge of the gospel) to the other (witnessing and living for Christ). The steps are conviction, regeneration, and sanctification. This scale helps us to see the process that a person goes through as he or she moves toward faith and then toward maturity.

Another way to communicate the process is to view it as levels of commitment. This is a simple process that your people can easily picture and understand. In this process, your strategy should reflect at least three levels of commitment (see fig. 9.2).

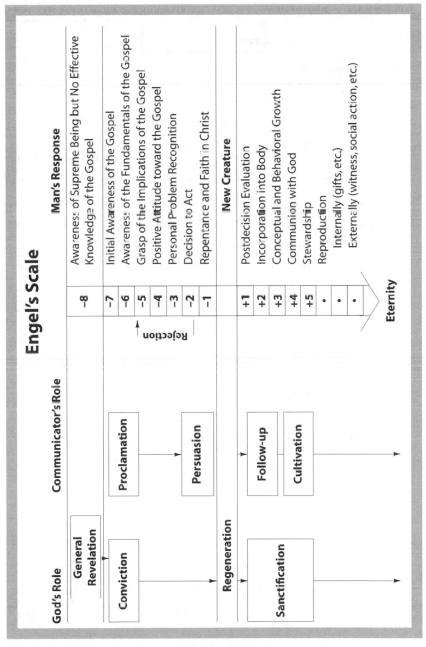

Figure 9.1. Engel's Scale

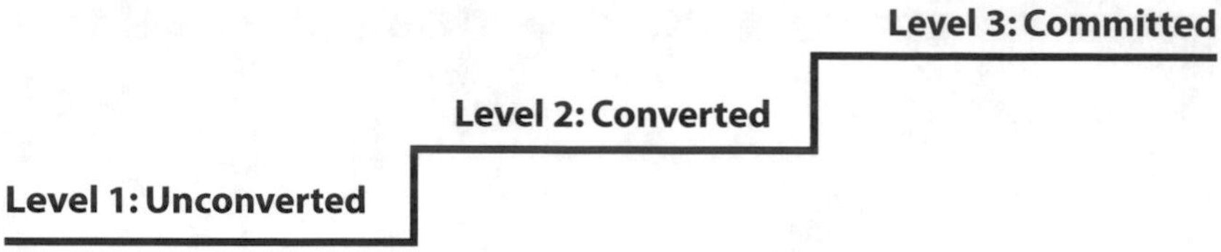

Figure 9.2. Levels of Commitment

Level one is where lost people are. They move to level two when they come to faith. Immediately after they come to faith, the church needs to help them move toward level three, maturity or Christlikeness. When people come to faith in Christ, they are responsible to move from one level to another. And it's the church's responsibility to help them in the process. Studies indicate that if someone doesn't come alongside a new convert, the chances are good that the convert will fall into nominal Christianity. The object of the church's strategy is to move them from the lowest level to the highest.

A Strategy Answers the Question, How?

Your mission strategy answers a critical question. It asks and answers the *how* question: How will this ministry, whether church or parachurch, accomplish its mission? Strategy is the ministry means to realize the ministry ends. If your mission is to take the hill, then your strategy is the *how* that will move you from the bottom to the top of that hill.

Since every church has a strategy reflected in its ministries and activities, when asked these questions, some people comment, "Oh, we already have a strategy." They are correct; however, the important question is, *Is it a good strategy?* The answer is simple: If it is accomplishing the mission of the ministry, then it's probably a good one. If the answer is, "Huh?" then you're in trouble.

At the beginning of the twenty-first century, the majority of the typical, traditional churches still cling to the three-to-thrive strategy that characterized most churches in the first half of the twentieth century. If you ask them how they are attempting to accomplish God's mission for them, they will show you their bulletin or a copy of their programs. My experience is that in much of America, especially urban America even in this century, strategy has not proved to be disciple friendly. You must regularly ask the *how* question so that your strategy is in tune with where the believers and unbelievers of this generation are.

STRATEGIES ON VARIOUS LEVELS

We can further define and refine the definition of a strategy by examining three different kinds of strategies.

Personal Strategy

In chapter 4 I pointed out that Christians should develop a personal life mission that answers the question, *What does God want to accomplish in and through my life?* The answer determines what you will do with your life and how you'll serve Christ. My personal ministry mission is to equip a new generation of leaders all over the world for significant, high-impact ministry in the twenty-first century. This mission statement helps me to make decisions that affect my life. When ministry opportunities come my way, I decide whether to pursue them based on my ministry mission. It also helps me to be proactive in ministry rather than reactive. Through God's strength and guidance, I shape my life and ministry rather than allow other people and other events to do so. Your personal strategy relates directly to your personal life mission. It's the process that determines how you will accomplish the mission that you've established for your life.

Organizational Strategy

Organizational strategy or congregational strategy (if your ministry is a church) is what this book is all about. Again, the organizational strategy is a mission strategy. It's the strategy that you have designed to accomplish your ministry mission. Therefore, it's the broad, umbrella strategy that all the other strategies in your ministry will fit under. All the other strategies must come under the organizational strategy and aid it in some way in accomplishing the ministry's mission and vision.

Departmental Strategy

I use the word *departmental* to include all the other strategies that exist in your ministry. Most organizations include ministries that fall under various departments or ministry areas. For example, a church may have a number of ministries such as Christian education, evangelism, worship, discipleship, small groups, and others. I argue in chapter 4 that each of these should have its own mission statement that falls within the parameters of the ministry's mission statement. Each must know what it's supposed to be doing or where it's going. For each department to accomplish its individual mission of evangelism, worship, and so forth, it must have its own unique strategy. Each must decide how it will lead people to worship, discipleship, and Christ. These are all ministrategies that fit within the mission strategy. If you cannot fit a departmental or ministry strategy under the mission strategy, then you must abandon it.

FIVE ELEMENTS OF AN EFFECTIVE STRATEGY

Finally, there are no less than five elements that make up an effective strategy, and each answers an important question. The following is an overview of these elements. I will develop them in the next chapter.

1. The first is the *ministry community*. You must develop a strategy to reach your community. It's the answer to the question, *To whom will we minister?* This includes not only where the church is located but the people to whom the church will minister. While it could be the houses immediately surrounding the church, more likely it will include much more. In a smaller

community, it might include an entire county or a town and its surrounding area. In a larger, metropolitan community, it might be a suburb or more. The church's ministry community will consist of its members and attendees plus those whom it hopes to reach with the gospel of Christ.

2. The second element is *disciple making*. You must design a strategy to make disciples. It answers the question, *What will we do for the people who live in our community?* The answer is to make disciples, consisting of winning them to faith in Christ and then moving them on to maturity. Most important to disciple making is determining what a mature disciple looks like and then assessing whether your current ministry activities are or will accomplish this. The result should be a clear pathway for making disciples in your church.

3. The third is *developing a ministry dream team*. You must design a strategy for developing your dram team. This answers the question, *Who will disciple the people who make up our community?* Your dream team for a church will consist of the pastor and any staff, a governing board (if your church has one), and the congregation whom Christ has called to do the work of the ministry (Eph. 4:11–13).

4. The fourth is the *ministry setting*. It consists of the church's facilities and location in the community. It answers the question, *Where will we locate ourselves to best make disciples of those in our ministry community?* You must develop a strategy to maximize your ministry setting.

5. The final element is *finances*. You must design a strategy to raise the necessary funds for ministry. This element addresses the question, *How will you fund the dream team's discipling of those in your community?* The area of financing tends to be a major weakness for most pastors. Many would rather not deal at all with having to raise funds, and few have, or ever implement, a strategy for financial stewardship. The problem is that, perhaps as much as anything, the lack of a financial strategy does not allow individual congregant's use of finances to reflect where he or she is spiritually.

QUESTIONS FOR REFLECTION, DISCUSSION, AND APPLICATION

1. A ministry may or may not have a mission statement. Does your ministry have one? If not, why not? Did it have one in the past? If so, what was it? What happened to it? How will you develop a strategy without a mission?

2. Every ministry has a strategy. What is yours? Is it a good strategy? How do you know? Does it move people from prebirth to maturity? If not, why not? If so, how?

3. Is it time to rethink your strategy? If you answered yes, then how do you know?

4. Do you have a personal ministry mission? If not, why not? If so, have you developed a strategy to implement your personal mission? If not, why not?

5. Do the different departments or areas within your ministry have mission statements? If so, do they have a strategy? Can they have a strategy without a mission? Explain.

10

The Development of a Strategy

How to Craft Your Strategy

God is using a number of excellent strategies in many large and small churches all across North America and abroad. The practice of pastors in smaller struggling churches is to go to a conference sponsored by one of these churches and learn the model in general and the strategy in particular. Next, they return to their troubled ministries and attempt to implement that model and that strategy. Unfortunately, it seldom works. The reason is that the pastor's community and culture is unlike that of the model church, and the pastors aren't similarly gifted as some of the pastors of these successful churches. And just as it takes all kinds of churches to reach all kinds of people, so it takes all kinds of strategies to reach all kinds of people.

This chapter is for leaders who desire to craft a mission strategy that's not endemic to some other part of the world or North America, but is their own. A good strategy consists of the following five steps. (Should you desire further, in-depth information on these five steps, see my book *Advanced Strategic Planning*.)[1]

STEP 1: IDENTIFY YOUR MINISTRY COMMUNITY

Your church's ministry community is its geographical sphere of spiritual influence. You need to know what that is. To discover this, you must ask and answer several community questions.

First, where is your community? Acts 1:8 addresses the boundaries of the ministry community for the Jerusalem church. They were to be witnesses in three geographical areas: Jerusalem, Judea and Samaria, and the uttermost parts of the world. To answer this question, you must discover the boundaries of your community. I refer to them as "soft boundaries" as these need to be flexible. The way you can determine your "soft boundaries" is to see how far you can drive away from the church in twenty-five minutes. Studies indicate that most people will not drive longer than twenty-five minutes to get to church. In a rural area you might reduce this to fifteen minutes. The drive time will also be affected by any man-made or natural boundaries such as a river, lake, or expressway. Another way to determine the boundaries is by miles traveled. I prefer to use ring studies of one, three, and five miles out from your church. One mile is your Jerusalem, three is your Judea and Samaria, and five miles is the world.

Second, who lives in your community? Now that you have your community's boundaries, you're ready to discover who lives in that community. To answer this question, you need to conduct a demographic study of your community. The primary tool for this study is the census. Keep in mind that the census is conducted every ten years. Thus, it will be more accurate when it's just been taken and less accurate as it approaches the next census time. The information that's most helpful to you will be the community's median age, level of education, ethnicity, income, marital status, and so on. You'll also need to gather any psychographic information that's available such as the community's needs, dreams, problems, values, attitudes, and so on. You may discover this information from a variety of sources such as the newspaper, area magazines, personal interviews and surveys, and professional agencies.

Once you've answered these questions, compare the results with your church. Are the various peoples in the community like those in your church? What do they have in common? What do they not have in common? Which people group is most like your people? They will be those whom you are most likely to reach.

Third, how many people will you reach in your community? Your answer to this question determines the size of your vision. I would suggest that you focus on those who are unchurched in your community. If you live in a small community, you could contact the churches in your community and get an idea of how many churched people there are. Then you could subtract this number from the total area population. Another option is to look up the area on the American Religion Data Archive (ARDA) at http://thearda.com. It will give you an idea of how many in the area are churched. Again, you can subtract that number from the total population. So how many can you reach? Most of the churches I work with settle on 10 percent of the total who are unchurched.

Fourth, whom will you reach? According to Scripture, you must be willing to reach anyone with the gospel, regardless of race, creed, age, or color. However, you may have a need to reach some people in particular. One example is young people. If a church finds that its average age is in the sixties or seventies, then it's in trouble and needs to do what it takes to reach a younger generation or begin to make funeral plans. Another example is men. Statistics make it quite clear that more women attend church than men. Regardless of the reason, churches should strategize to reach men in particular.

Fifth, what kind of church will reach your community? Based on your demographic and psychographic work, answer the following questions:

- What kind of pastor will best reach your community?
- What kind of staff will best reach your community?
- What style of worship will impact your community?

- What kind of congregants will appeal to your community (warm, friendly, accepting, etc.)?
- What kind of facilities will appeal to your community?

STEP 2: MAKE MATURE DISCIPLES

Now that you have an idea of whom you are going to reach—your target community—you need to determine how they'll move from wherever they are (lost or saved) to where Christ wants them to be—mature disciples. You must design your pathway for making disciples. How might you accomplish this? Pursue the following three goals:

First, develop your ministry mission. Most likely you've already done so earlier in this book. Of course, your mission will be an expression of the Great Commission (Matt. 28:19–20; Mark 16:15, etc.).

Second, identify the characteristics of a mature disciple. If a mature disciple were to walk through the entryway to your church facility, what would he or she look like? If you carefully examine these characteristics in the New Testament, you'll find there are many. Several characteristics, however, will fall under certain general categories. Under the category of worship, for example, a mature disciple would regularly participate in communion, prayer, and giving. I believe the New Testament identifies at least five critical categories in Luke's church progress report in Acts 2:41–47: evangelism, worship, fellowship, service, and the teaching and application of Scripture.

Third, design a disciple maturing process. The goal is to identify the necessary ministry activities that will help your people embrace in their lives the characteristics if a mature disciple. You may already have these in place or you may need to develop some. How can you know? I have developed a maturity matrix that will help you determine this (see chart 10.1). Here's how it works. Place your characteristics of maturity along the top of the horizontal axis. Then place your current, major ministry activities (such essentials as the worship-preaching event, Sunday school, small groups, and any others) on the vertical axis. These are the activities necessary for your people to embrace the characteristics.

Characteristics of Maturity
(Ministry Ends)

	Conversion (Evangelism)	Community (Fellowship)	Celebration (Worship)	Cultivation (Teaching)	Contribution (Service)
Develop a relationship with a lost person					
Share a verbal witness with a lost person					
Attend a worship service					
Join a Sunday school					
Join a small group					

Ministry Activities (Ministry Means)

Chart 10.1. Maturity Matrix

The key is that every activity support the implementation of at least one of the characteristics.

STEP 3: BUILD A MINISTRY DREAM TEAM

It's imperative that you have a strategy to develop a ministry dream team. Though the New Testament doesn't prescribe that we do ministry in teams, most of its examples of effective ministry are in a team context. Jesus ministered through a small team of ragtag disciples. And we all associate men such as Barnabas, Mark, Silas, and others with the ministry of Paul. Then Paul provides us with a body metaphor for team ministry in 1 Corinthians 12:12–31. Keep in mind that your ministry will only be as good as the people who minister and lead it.

A church's dream team is made up of at least three groups. The first group is a wise, godly governing board whom I refer to as the leaders of leaders. Most churches have such a board and call them elders, deacons, trustees, overseers, or some other name. I'm not sure that Scripture prescribes board ministry, but it's certainly a wise approach to church leadership. My view is that these boards lead at the top level of church leadership and function as leaders in several ways. First, they can pray for the church. They can monitor or oversee the church in four areas: its spiritual condition, its biblical and doctrinal integrity, its direction (the Great Commission), and the pastor's leadership. Second, the board will have to make lots of decisions that affect the church and its leadership. I would argue that the best way to do this is to follow the policy-making approach that I present in my book *Leading Leaders*.[2] Finally, the board functions to advise the pastor as he or she leads the ministry. Because of the responsibilities of board members, their qualifications should be high. My own view is that 1 Timothy 3:1–7 and Titus 1:5–9 are the first-century qualifications for pastors. However, I believe that the governing board should meet the same qualifications.

The second group in your dream team is the pastor and any staff. The staff you want are the people you dream about when you find yourself meaningfully involved up to your elbows in ministry. Several considerations should be kept in mind when recruiting the members of such a team. First is character. Like the governing board, the pastor and staff should be godly people who put the Savior first in their lives. Second is timing. We usually wait until we're overwhelmed with some aspect of ministry before we add a new staff person. Instead, I would challenge you to think about adding that person when you first have the need for them. Third is balancing in-reach with outreach. Most church staff teams are in-reach oriented. Thus, we shouldn't be surprised when the church plateaus and begins to die because there's little or no outreach. Attempt to have one or more outreach positions on your staff.

In addition to the above recruiting considerations are three cs: character, competence, and chemistry. I've already commented on the importance of character. In addition to character, it's vital to the church that the staff person be most competent at what he or she does. Make sure you know what you want that staff person to do, develop a job or ministry description, and then hire the best person available. Most often the best person is in ministry somewhere as opposed to out looking for a position. Thus, you may wind up in the regrettable position of hiring them away from another church. The third c is chemistry. A person can meet all the character qualifications and be the most competent staff person in his or her field, but not mesh with the rest of the staff team emotionally. The same can be true of that person's theology or doctrine as well as his or her core values, mission, and vision. We refer to this essential element of team ministry as chemistry. If potential recruits don't get along with your people and don't align doctrinally and philosophically, then don't hire them. Should you make that mistake, you'll find that they'll only last a short time before they move on to "greener pastures."

The third element of your dream team is the congregation. Scripture is explicit that it's the congregation who is to do the work of the ministry, and this is necessary for your church to mature (Eph. 4:11–13). Unfortunately for the church of Jesus Christ, Satan has convinced the majority of congregations in North America that ministry is the responsibility of the pastor and staff. My view is that this false approach to ministry has brought the church to its knees in terms of what it could accomplish. What's the solution? The leadership needs to craft and embrace a congregational mobilization system. Such a ministry would consist of three phases. The first is the discovery phase where people in the congregation discover their divine designs that consist of their natural and spiritual gifts, passions, and temperaments. Next is the consulting phase where a trained lay or staff person answers any questions and confirms or corrects a congregant's understanding of his or her design. Third is the placement phase. This is where the ministry places its congregants into various positions of service that fit or match with each individual's divine design.

STEP 4: DETERMINE THE BEST MINISTRY SETTING

Next, a church must develop a strategy to maximize its setting. A church's setting is anywhere that its ministry takes place. It's where your church delivers ministry. It's where your mobilized members make disciples. Most likely this is anywhere in your ministry community. I want to focus in this section, however, specifically on the church's facilities and property. One issue that churches must face is determining the best location for their ministries. Often a church is planted in what seems like an ideal location in suburbia, only to wake up twenty or thirty years later to discover that the community has changed and the people it formerly ministered to have relocated, and the new residents aren't interested in the church. In determining where it should locate, a church needs to assess the following issues. First, where are your current members and attendees located in relationship to the church main facility? If they have relocated to some other part of the community and are driving over twenty-five minutes to get to church, it's only a matter of time before you'll lose them to a church that's nearer to where they're located. Second, where are the people located whom you'll most likely reach with the gospel? If they live somewhere else and outside a reasonable driving time, then your chances of reaching them are slim. In both of these situations, you would be wise to relocate the church for the most effective ministry.

Some churches find themselves in a good location to minister to people but growing to the point where they have little if any room. This may necessitate a relocation somewhere within the community but in a larger facility. Before a church embarks on such a relocation, I would suggest it offer multiple services. When you reach 80 percent capacity in the first service due to growth, start a second service. It could be the same kind of worship service or an alternative service that could expand the church's outreach even further. In addition, I would suggest that you begin to consider expanding your facilities or looking for other facilities if you've maximized yours. When the second service reaches 80 percent capacity, I would start a third service and begin to remodel your current facilities or begin construction on new facilities. If you time it well, by the time you've maximized your third service, you've finished building and are ready to meet in your expanded or new facilities. I wouldn't recommend going to a fourth service because of the havoc it reeks on the Christian education program and worship side of your ministry.

Finally, your church should consider the following factors regarding your facilities:

1. *Appearance.* Does the church look run-down? Sometimes this happens and the congregation is hardly aware of it. They get used to their situation and don't view their facilities through visitors' eyes.

2. *Church size.* Is the facility big enough for the congregation? If not, then pursue what I've suggested in the last paragraph. If it's too big, you may want to consider a revitalization of your ministry before you take the step of relocating to a smaller facility.

3. *The grounds.* Is the grass mowed and are the weeds pulled? If not, potential visitors may shun attending your church.

4. *Parking.* Do you have adequate parking for the number of people who attend and for those who might attend in the future (your targeted people in your community)?

5. *Visitors.* Do you need to designate some of the spaces closer to the front of the building for visitors?

6. *Signage.* Would a visitor know where the nursery is or where the bathrooms are located? How about Sunday school classes?

7. *Cleanliness.* For many, cleanliness is next to godliness. How clean are your bathrooms? How clean are the nursery and other children's areas?

STEP 5: RAISE THE NECESSARY FINANCES

Last, the church needs a strategy to raise the necessary finances for doing ministry. My experience is that strategic, gifted leaders are on top of their church's finances. Thus, if the thought of raising and working with your church's finances are a turnoff, maybe you need to rethink your leadership gift. Whether we like it or not, and many don't, finances are an important aspect of ministry. Ministry costs money! And the way your people handle their finances is also a reflection of your ministry in their lives. In this section, I would like to briefly address three financial questions.

Who is responsible for managing the ministry's finances? The answer is the buck stops with the senior pastor or only leader. Bill Hybels writes, "Be as theological as you want to be, but the church will never reach her full redemptive potential until a river of financial sources starts flowing in her direction. And like it or not, it is the leader's job to create that river and to manage it wisely."[3] A leader should have a theology of stewardship and finances, and is responsible to communicate that theology. In our culture congregations also look to their leader for his or her leadership in this area. If he or she is negligent in taking care of finances, it will have a considerable impact on his or her church.

How much money does the leader need to raise? The answer is found in the budget. A leader's management of the finances also includes working with the budget. The leaders plays an important role in developing a strategic budget for that church and then using it as a guide to the various financial aspects of that ministry. Most budgets break down into four areas. The following are those areas and the percentage of the budget assigned to each in growing, spiritually healthy churches. Compare your budget to these figures and see how you're doing:

- Missions and evangelism: 10–15 percent
- Personnel: 40–60 percent (lower in larger churches; higher in smaller ones)

- Programming: 20 percent
- Facilities: 20–25 percent

How will the leader raise these necessary funds? Yes, it's the people who are supposed to give liberally but, again, the leader leads. How might God use a specific leader to raise the necessary funds for a vibrant, spiritually healthy ministry?

1. A leader must have a biblical theology of finances that guides him or her in not only preaching but in the handling of all aspects of the finances.
2. A leader must regularly cast the church's vision. Ministries that cast vision well are excellent at raising ministry funds.
3. A leader must implement a churchwide stewardship ministry. This would include the following:
   - preaching on finances for one month each year
   - implementing stewardship in the Sunday school classes and small groups
   - explaining the church's giving expectations to new members
   - counseling for those who struggle in handling their finances
   - a ministry of deferred giving
   - quarterly workshops on financial planning
4. A leader must constantly communicate with the congregation—especially in the area of the church's finances.
5. A leader needs to conduct periodic capital campaigns. These campaigns stretch people and help them to see how they can increase their giving to God.
6. A leader needs to cultivate the church's gifted givers. Some pastors cultivate those in the church with the gifts of leading and evangelism as well as other gifts. Why not those with the gift of giving?

Should you desire more information on how to lead your ministry in the area of finances, see *Money Matters in Church*. This is a book that my pastor, Steve Stroope, and I wrote specifically for pastors.[4]

QUESTIONS FOR REFLECTION, DISCUSSION, AND APPLICATION

1. Who are some of the people that make up your ministry community? What are their needs, values, dreams, desires? Who in your community might you reach out to? How many unchurched people are in your community? How many of them might your church lead to Christ? Is this 10 percent?

2. Have you developed a ministry mission statement? If not, why not? What are the characteristics or traits of a mature disciple in your church? What are your primary ministry activities that help your people embrace these characteristics? Do you have at least one major activity for each characteristic?

3. Does your church have a governing board? What is its role in the church's ministry? What kind of character requirements does the church require of the staff? What is the competence level of your staff as a whole? Individually? Does anyone on the staff show poor chemistry? Do you have a mobilization process in place to help your people find places of ministry in the church?

4. Does your church have a good location? How do you know? How far does the typical member or attendee drive to get to church? Is this good or bad? Do your members still live within a reasonable drive time of the church? Is this the same for those in the community you might target? Does your church need to relocate? Why, and how do you know?

5. If you're a pastor, what are your feelings about raising and managing the church's finances? What training, if any, have you received in this vital area of ministry? Does the author's recommended budget percentiles match those of your church? Do you have a theology of

stewardship that addresses what the Bible says about finances? Do you have a strategy of stewardship? Why or why not? If you do, how are you implementing it in your church? If you don't, would the author's strategy work for you? Why or why not?

Appendix A

Acadiana Community Church:
Credo and Doctrinal Statement

OUR VALUES

We Value Full Devotion to Christ and His Cause

We believe that wholehearted devotion to Jesus Christ is not only the biblical norm for the believer, but that anything less is sin in God's eyes. Full devotion should be expected of and encouraged by every believer in the community.

We Value Being a Biblically Functioning Community

We believe that the first priority of any church is to be and do the things that God expects of a biblically functioning community, that is devotion to the Word, worship, and walk of God.

We Value Having a Great Commission Vision

We believe that if we are to be the church, we must have God's vision for the church, which is ultimately to glorify the Father by continuing

Used by permission.

Christ's earthly ministry of seeking, saving, and serving. We do this when we make disciples by reaching and teaching the unchurched to be fully devoted followers of Jesus Christ.

We Value Culturally Adapting Ministry

We believe that while the truth of God's Word never changes, the culture in which we are called to apply these unchanging principles of truth is ever changing. Therefore, we must understand our culture and minister the truth of God's Word in the most effective way possible, even if this means laying aside some of the man-made traditions of the church.

We Value Lost People as God Values Lost People

We believe that lost people are valuable to God and therefore should be equally valuable to us. We spend time and energy on that which we value; therefore, we should spend time and energy pursuing lost people as Christ did when He was on this earth.

We Value Biblical Culturally Relevant Evangelism

We believe that evangelism begins with our willingness to befriend and build relationships with lost people. We also believe that it is the work of the Spirit of God to bring people into His kingdom. Our responsibility is to be faithful in showing God's love to the lost through caring relationships and to be ready to share the gospel with them through a variety of methods as the Holy Spirit gives opportunity.

We Value Authentic, Holistic Worship

We believe that man was made to worship God and that a primary responsibility of the individual and church corporately is to worship God in spirit and truth. We believe this worship should involve the whole person: body, emotions, intellect, and will. We also believe this worship is a lifestyle of obedience, not simply a once a week experience.

We Value Equipping and Mobilizing Members to Minister

We believe that everyone in the body of Christ has been uniquely designed to serve God. This divine design involves personality, spiritual giftedness, experience, and passion. We believe that it is the responsibility of the church corporately to equip, encourage, and actively help the individual believer find the place where God has designed him or her to serve in the body of Christ. We understand that this place of service may or may not be within the traditional programs of the church.

We Value Strong, Servant Leadership

We believe that Christ is ultimately the only head of the church, but that He has chosen to function through human leaders in the local church. We believe that these human leaders must meet the biblical qualifications of leadership. They must have godly character, biblical vision, and influence. We believe leadership must be team leadership if it is to be biblical and effective in our culture. But we also realize that, as with all biblical teams, this team leadership must be led by a visionary leader of leaders. Leadership must model the leadership of Christ in that it is both strong leadership and servant leadership. Hence, we believe that the church should be led by strong, servant team leadership led by a strong servant leader of leaders.

DOCTRINAL STATEMENT

The Bible

We believe that the original manuscripts of the Old and New Testament comprise the full, word-for-word, truthful, inerrant Word of God, which is the supreme and final authority in doctrine and practice (Isa. 40:8; 2 Tim. 3:16–17; Heb. 4:12; 2 Peter 1:20–21).

The Trinity

We believe in one God eternally existing in three equal persons—Father,

Son, and Holy Spirit, who have the same nature and attributes but who are distinct in office and activity (Deut. 6:4; Isa. 48:16; Jer. 10:10; Matt. 28:19; John 10:30; Acts 5:3–4; 2 Cor. 13:14; Heb. 1:8).

The Father

We believe that as eternal Father, He is the Father of all men in the non-salvation, Creator-creature sense, the Father of the nation Israel, the Father of the Lord Jesus Christ, and the spiritual Father of all who believe in Christ. He is the author of salvation, the One who sent the Son, and the disciplinarian of His children (Exod. 4:22; Ps. 2:7–9; John 5:37; Acts 17:29; Gal. 3:26; Eph. 1:3–6; Heb. 12:9; 1 Peter 1:3).

The Person and Work of Jesus Christ

We believe Jesus Christ is God incarnate, conceived by the Holy Spirit, born of a virgin, completely God and completely man. We believe in His preexistence, His sinless life, His substitutionary atonement, His bodily resurrection from the grave, His ascension into heaven, and His bodily return from heaven (Luke 1:35; John 1:1, 14, 18; Rom. 3:24–26; 4:25; Eph. 4:11–16; 1 Thess. 4:13–18; Heb. 1:3; 7:23–25; 1 Peter 1:3–5; 1 John 2:1–2).

The Holy Spirit

We believe that the Holy Spirit regenerates, indwells, baptizes, seals, and bestows spiritual gifts upon all believers at the time of their conversion. Experientially, He fills, teaches, leads, assures, and prays for believers (John 14:26; 16:6–15; Acts 1:5; 2:1–4; 11:1–18; Rom. 8:14–16, 26–27; 1 Cor. 6:19; 12:7–11, 13; Eph. 1:13–14; 5:18; 2 Thess. 2:1–10; Titus 3:5).

Man and Sin

We believe man was created in the image of God; that he sinned in Adam and thereby incurred both physical and spiritual death (separation from God); is now a sinner, by nature and by choice; and is in need of salvation

(Gen. 1:1, 27; 2:17; 3:1–19; Isa. 14:12–14; Luke 20:36; John 1:1–3; 8:44; 12:31; Rom. 5:12–21; Eph. 2:1–3; Col. 1:16–17; Heb. 1:13–14; 2:5–8, 14; 1 Peter 2:4; Jude 6; Rev. 20:10).

Salvation

We believe in salvation by grace through faith in Jesus Christ's substitutionary payment for our sins, not based on human merit, works, or religious ceremony. We believe that anyone who has placed their faith in Christ is eternally secure, has everlasting life, will not come into condemnation, and shall never perish. We believe that assurance comes to the believer from three primary sources: trusting the Word of God's promises, the witness of the Holy Spirit, and a persevering walk with the Lord (Dan. 12:1–2; Matt. 25:31–46; John 1:12; 2:3, 16; 3:16; 5:24; 10:28–29; 11:25–26; 2 Cor. 5:17–21; Eph. 2:8–9; Titus 3:4–7; Rom. 8:28–39; 1 John 4:11–13; Jude 1; Rev. 20:12–15).

The Church

We believe in the church, both universally and locally, as the spiritual body of which Christ is the Head, and in the practices of water baptism of believers and the Lord's Supper as the ordinances of the local church (Matt. 16:18; Acts 1:5; 11:15; 1 Cor. 12:13; Eph. 1:22–23; 4:11–16; 5:22–33; Col. 1:18).

The Great Commission

We believe that those whom God has saved are sent into the world by Christ as He was by the Father. Those so sent are ambassadors, commissioned to go make disciples and make Christ known to the whole world. We also believe that everyone should have an opportunity to carefully examine the facts about Christ and have a chance to make an intelligent decision about Him (Matt. 28:18–20; John 15:17–18, 20–21; Acts 1; Rom. 10:14–15; 2 Cor. 5:18–20; Col. 4:2–6; 2 Tim. 2:14–26).

Eternity

We believe in the physical resurrection of the human body (at the second coming of Christ), in the eternal conscious existence of all individuals in either heaven or hell, and in the rewards of the saved and the punishment of the lost for eternity (1 Cor. 15; Luke 16:19–31; 2 Cor. 5:8–10; 1 Cor. 3:11–15).

Appendix B

Church Credos

THE JERUSALEM CHURCH, JERUSALEM, ISRAEL
Core Values

1. We value expository teaching (Acts 2:42–43).
2. We value fellowship (Acts 2:42).
3. We value prayer (Acts 2:42).
4. We value biblical community (Acts 2:44–46).
5. We value praise and worship (Acts 2:47).
6. We value evangelism (Acts 2:47).

FELLOWSHIP BIBLE CHURCH, DALLAS, TEXAS

We have ten core values that guide us. These values describe the culture that we seek to create at FBC. We aspire to be

1. Biblically Faithful: We make Scripture the final authority rather than church tradition. We seek to be innovative and flexible as long as we do not violate Scripture.

Used by permission.

2. Culturally Relevant: We try to adapt our ministry to current needs and trends in American life, without compromising biblical absolutes. We attempt to communicate the good news of Jesus Christ to American society in ways it can understand.

3. Grace Oriented: We emphasize God's unconditional acceptance and full forgiveness through Jesus Christ. We attempt to motivate people through love and thankfulness rather than guilt, shame, and duty.

4. Seeker Sensitive: We know that many who are not yet committed to Christ are attracted to our ministry; therefore, we desire to create a non-threatening environment in which they are free to explore the Christian faith at their own pace.

5. Growth Responsive: We appreciate the advantages of a small, intimate congregation, but also feel we should respond to the numerical growth that often results from reaching out to those who are exploring Christianity. We do not set a particular limit on the size of our congregation, but trust God to show the church leadership what our facilities should be and how best to utilize them.

6. Relationally Centered: We stress healthy relationships among Christians. We emphasize small groups as a primary means for Christians to care for each other, develop friendships, and share their lives.

7. People Developing: We seek to help people grow spiritually. We provide biblical instruction, and we encourage believers to discover and exercise their spiritual gifts.

8. Family Affirming: We seek to provide an atmosphere that strengthens marriages and families. We are committed to strong youth and children's programs.

9. Simply Structured: We assign the ultimate leadership of the church to elders and the daily operations of the church to paid staff, who are responsible to set up effective programs.

10. Cross Culturally Effective: We reach beyond our own culture as we seek to have an effective impact on other cultures with the gospel.

LAKEVIEW COMMUNITY CHURCH, CEDAR HILL, TEXAS

This statement of principles clarifies the attitudes and approaches that will be encouraged in the ministries of Lakeview Community Church. Most of these are not biblical absolutes, but they represent our understanding of how to most effectively accomplish our purpose.

1. A Commitment to Relevant Bible Exposition

   We believe that the Bible is God's inspired Word, the authoritative and trustworthy rule of faith and practice for Christians. The Bible is both timeless and timely, relevant to the common needs of all people at all times and to the specific problems of contemporary living. Therefore, we are committed to equipping Christians, through the preaching and teaching of God's Word, to follow Christ in every sphere of life.

2. A Commitment to Prayer

   We believe that God desires his people to pray and that he hears and answers prayer (Matt. 7:7–11; James 5:13–18). Therefore, the ministries and activities of this church will be characterized by a reliance on prayer in their conception, planning, and execution.

3. A Commitment to Lay Ministry

   We believe that the primary responsibility of the pastor(s) and teachers in the local church is to "prepare God's people for works of service" (Eph. 4:12). Therefore, the ministry of Lakeview Community Church will be placed as much as possible in the hands of nonvocational workers. This will be accomplished through training opportunities and through practices that encourage lay initiation, leadership, responsibility, and authority in the various ministries of the church.

4. A Commitment to Small Groups

   We are committed to small-group ministry as one of the most effective means of building relationships, stimulating spiritual growth, and developing leaders.

5. An Appreciation for Creativity and Innovation

In today's rapidly changing world, forms and methods must be continually evaluated and, if necessary, altered to fit new conditions. While proven techniques should not be discarded at a whim, we encourage creativity and innovation, flexibility and adaptability. We are more concerned with effectiveness in ministry than with adherence to tradition.

6. A Commitment to Excellence

We believe that the God of our salvation deserves the best we have to offer. The Lord himself is a God of excellence, as shown by the beauty of creation; further, he gave the best that he had, his only Son, for us (Rom. 8:32). Paul exhorts servants, in whatever they do, to "work at it with all your heart, as working for the Lord, not for men" (Col. 3:23). Therefore, in the ministries and activities of Lakeview Community Church we will seek to maintain a high standard of excellence to the glory of God. This will be achieved when every person is exercising his or her God-given spiritual gift to the best of his or her ability (1 Cor. 12).

7. A Commitment to Growth

Although numerical growth is not necessarily a sign of God's blessing, and is not a sufficient goal in itself, we believe that God desires for us to reach as many people as possible with the life-changing message of Jesus Christ. Therefore, we will pursue methods and policies that will facilitate numerical growth, without compromising in any way our integrity or our commitment to biblical truth.

THE VILLAGE CHURCH, HIGHLAND VILLAGE, TEXAS

The core values of the Village Church are Truth, Christian Spirituality, Community, Foot-Washing, and Missional Living. These values serve as the foundation of our ministry and hopefully capture in a word God's thematic purposes found in Scripture. The expression and extension for each value along with its corresponding virtue can be found below.

Truth

Expression: "What is truth?" Pilate asks Jesus this question in John 18. Truth was standing right in front of him, and he did not see it. Truth is a paradox of realities: It is both complex and simple, static and dynamic, Truth is a Person. Although we cannot capture Truth in a sentence, we find its essence in the Triune God. So, Truth is found in the Person of Jesus. He is the Truth, and the Truth sets us free (John 14:6; 8:32). God's self-disclosure to humanity is found in a sacred compilation of various works known as the Bible. God has given us 66 books (39 Old Testament, 27 New Testament) written in three languages (Hebrew, Greek, and a bit of Aramaic), over a period of more than a thousand years, by over 40 authors on three continents (Asia, Africa, and Europe). Authors include kings, peasants, philosophers, fishermen, poets, statesmen, scholars, etc. Books cover history, sermons, letters, a hymn book, and a love song. There are geographical surveys, architectural specifications, travel diaries, family trees, and numerous legal documents. It covers hundred of controversial subjects with amazing unity. It is the best-selling book of all time and is now available in over 3,000 languages. It is our guide to Truth . . . our compass to the Triune God. The Bible is an essential and infallible record of God's self-disclosure to humanity. These Scriptures are fully inspired by God. We express Truth through grace.

Extension: We search the Scriptures to be introduced to the Triune God and discover the Truth that sets us free. We desire to couple Truth with grace in hopes that we might also introduce non-believers or re-introduce de-churched believers to this same God. We want to extend Truth to a culture desperately seeking answers, hope, and meaning.

Virtue: Grace

The apostle John writes in his gospel, "And the Word became flesh, and dwelt among us, and we saw His glory, glory as of the only begotten from the Father, full of grace and truth . . . For of His fullness we have all received, and grace upon grace. For the Law was given through Moses; grace and truth were realized through Jesus Christ" (John 1:14, 16–17 NASB). The value of Truth corresponds with the virtue of grace. Unfortunately, the message of Truth has been dismissed largely on the basis of the disposition of the messenger. As we express and extend Truth to our community we desire to envelop it with the virtue of grace. Our Savior is the model for this mixture.

Christian Spirituality

Expression: Truth without meaning is empty, worthless, and most of all dangerous. We need meaning. We want Truth in motion and Truth lived out. When love collides with the heart, it creates. We express Christian Spirituality through love.

Extension: Christian Spirituality is one way Truth works itself out in real life. Prayer, fasting, art, poetry, drama, solitude, meditation, music, writing—these are some of the aspects of Christian Spirituality. Our faith is not merely intellectual. It stirs, creates, motivates, and hurts. It is innovative and spontaneous, beautiful and messy. We value and encourage the outworking of Truth in our community through the myriad of forms Christian Spirituality can take.

Virtue: Love

The apostle Paul writes in his letters to the Corinthians, "Let all that you do be done in love; For the love of Christ controls us" (1 Cor. 16:14; 2 Cor. 5:14). The value of Christian Spirituality corresponds with the virtue of love. Since this value includes the essence of the Christian life as seen in creativity, discipline, work, and play, it is only fitting that the virtue of love would blanket this value. Love is the primary virtue of the Scriptures and the one that demonstrates to the world the evidence of Christ in us, the hope of glory (Col. 1:27).

Community

Expression: Throughout the Bible, community is a major theme. Beginning with His first creation, continuing with Israel and the New Testament Church, God always calls out a people for Himself. Even when the Jews were in captivity and dispersed among enemy nations, they organized themselves into groups that ultimately formed synagogues where they could serve one another and carry out their beliefs. In Acts 2, the first-century church met in temple courts (Sunday morning worship) and in house-to-house (home group) settings. These new church communities began as small groups, just as Jesus had modeled with the Twelve (Mark 3:14; Luke 6:12–19). There are over 50 biblical "one another's" that admonish us to be closely involved with a few others (small groups) in order that we might learn and imitate attitudes and behaviors that characterize God's household—the community of believers. We express Community through authenticity.

Extension: Small groups are intentional efforts to create an atmosphere conducive for believers and non-believers to grow in their understanding and application of God's direction in their lives. Small groups help create biblical community. We value genuine, real, and authentic relationships.

Virtue: Authenticity

The apostle Paul writes in his epistle to the Ephesians, "Having put away falsehood, let each one of you speak truth with his neighbor, for we are members of one another" (Eph. 4:25). The value of Community corresponds with the virtue of authenticity. Falsehood can be found in our speech or in our presentation of self. Webster defines authenticity as "true to one's own personality, spirit or character." Authenticity, which is very near to the virtue of honesty, is the fertile soil in which the graces grow. Community thrives when people are authentic and genuine, yet it is misleading and disingenuous when authenticity is sparse.

Foot-Washing

Expression: At The Village, we desire to follow our Lord's example to wash each other's feet. That is, we are to serve one another in the church. But our service extends to those in our community as well. Foot-washing expresses itself in a myriad of ways from changing diapers in the nursery, mowing lawns for widows, providing childcare for single moms, parking cars for weekend worship, serving meals to the hungry, or attending to the needs of the less fortunate. The Son of Man did not come to be served, but to serve. We express service through humility.

Extension: Jesus demonstrated for us the necessity of serving one another when He washed the disciple's feet, but He also shared the story about the Good Samaritan to open our eyes to the needs of the world. Jesus radically taught that our neighbor is anyone in need, regardless of social status, race, or even religious preference. We are called to wash the feet of our neighbors in order to demonstrate the rich compassion of our Lord. We desire to mobilize our membership for life-affirming outreach and ministries of mercy within our community and beyond. We desire that our members show compassion daily for the widow, the orphan, the poor, and the outcast. We are to ask ourselves, "Who can I be a neighbor to?" Those who follow the way of Jesus will be known for their love towards others. We can wash one another's feet by serving in home groups, greeting during the weekends or facilitating a group in the children's ministry. Outside of the needs of our church body provides a wealth of opportunities to serve our neighbors. We can be a part of transforming a neighborhood in Dallas, volunteering at the pregnancy center, or getting involved in the Local Missions Ministry.

Virtue: Humility

The apostle Paul writes in his epistle to the Philippians, "Do nothing from rivalry or conceit, but in humility count others more significant than yourselves. Let each of you look not only to his own interests, but also to the interests of others. Have this mind among yourselves, which is yours in Christ Jesus, who, though he was in the form of God, did not count equality with God a thing to be grasped, but made himself nothing, taking the form of a servant" (Phil. 2:3–7 esv). The value of Foot-Washing corresponds to the virtue of humility. Jesus modeled humility in His incarnation, His life, and His death. Humility is the foundational virtue of the Scriptures. It is the basis of our confession of our need for salvation in Christ. It is the basis of our worship as we see God's great worth. It is the basis of our service as we see others [as] better than ourselves.

Missional Living

Expression: We want to be intentional about life, to live life on purpose. Acts 17:26 says that "He [God] made from one man every nation of mankind to live on all the face of the earth, having determined their appointed periods and the boundaries of their habitation" (esv). This means that God was intentional about our lives. He placed us in neighborhoods, work places, classrooms, gyms, and coffee shops on purpose. Life is not a random accident; rather, God designed it with intention and purpose. We express Missional Living through obedience.

Extension: We want to live the way of Jesus in front of the audience that God has given us. We love, serve, and care for those that God has "determined" us to be around in the hopes they will see Jesus in us, hear us speak of Him often, and be drawn to Him. We extend our lives missionally when we introduce or re-introduce our neighbors, co-workers, family, and friends to the great and glorious gospel of Jesus Christ.

Virtue: Obedience

Our Lord Jesus declared that "All authority in heaven and on earth has been given to me. Go therefore and make disciples of all nations, baptizing them in the name of the Father and of the Son and of the Holy Spirit, teaching them to observe all that I have commanded you. And behold, I am with you always, to the end of the age" (Matt. 28:18–20

ESV). The value of Missional Living corresponds with the virtue of obedience. The Great Commission is the basis of our mission and is not an option for the believer in Christ. Christ has called His people to obedience in His mission. Obedience is not a popular word in our culture, but joy is found in obedience. Jesus made the issue clear in the gospel of John: "If you love me, you will keep my commandments . . . Whoever has my commandments and keeps them, he it is who loves me. And he who loves me will be loved by my Father, and I will love him and manifest myself to him . . . If anyone loves me, he will keep my word, and my Father will love him, and we will come to him and make our home with him" (John 14:15, 21, 23 ESV). Jesus did not leave obedience up to us alone, but He provided His Holy Spirit, who leads us, guides us, teaches us, and conforms us into the image of Christ. Obedience is joint work of the believer and the Spirit.

WILLOW CREEK COMMUNITY CHURCH, SOUTH BARRINGTON, ILLINOIS

1. We believe that anointed teaching is the catalyst for transformation in individuals' lives and in the church.

    This includes the concept of teaching for life change—Romans 12:7; 2 Timothy 3:16–17; James 1:23–25.

2. We believe that lost people matter to God, and therefore, ought to matter to the church.

    This includes the concepts of relational evangelism and evangelism as a process—Luke 5:30–32; Luke 15; Matthew 18:14.

3. We believe that the church should be culturally relevant while remaining doctrinally pure.

    This includes the concept of sensitively relating to our culture through our facility, printed materials, and use of the arts—1 Corinthians 9:19–23.

4. We believe that Christ-followers should manifest authenticity and yearn for continuous growth.

    This includes the concepts of personal authenticity, character, and wholeness—Ephesians 4:25–26, 32; Hebrews 12:1; Philippians 1:6.

5. We believe that a church should operate as a unified community of servants with men and women stewarding their spiritual gifts.

    This includes the concepts of unity, servanthood, spiritual gifts, and ministry calling—1 Corinthians 12 and 14; Romans 12; Ephesians 4; Psalm 133:1.

6. We believe that loving relationships should permeate every aspect of church life.

    This includes the concepts of love-driven ministry, ministry accomplished in teams and relationship building—1 Corinthians 13; Nehemiah 3; Luke 10:1; John 13:34–35.

7. We believe that life-change happens best in small groups.

    This includes the concepts of discipleship, vulnerability, and accountability—Luke 6:12–13; Acts 2:44–47.

8. We believe that excellence honors God and inspires people.

    This includes the concepts of evaluation, critical review, intensity and excellence—Colossians 3:17; Malachi 1:6–14; Proverbs 27:17.

9. We believe that churches should be led by men and women with leadership gifts.

    This includes the concepts of empowerment, servant leadership, strategic focus, and intentionality—Nehemiah 1–2; Romans 12:8; Acts 6:2–5.

10. We believe that the pursuit of full devotion to Christ and His cause is normal for every believer.

    This includes the concepts of stewardship, servanthood, downward mobility, and the pursuit of kingdom goals—1 Kings 11:4; Philippians 2:1–11; 2 Corinthians 8:7.

WOODDALE CHURCH, EDEN PRAIRIE, MINNESOTA

The purpose of Wooddale Church is to honor God by making more disciples for Jesus Christ.

Values are what Wooddale Church lives by to fulfill our purpose.

God-Centered

Wooddale Church exists for God. In every person and program God is first, God is experienced, and God is to be pleased. We delight to constantly have God on our minds and in our conversations. Wooddale Church is the people and place where God is experienced. Public gathering to worship is a primary expression. Personal godly living is an equally important expression.

Bible-Based

Wooddale Church lives by the Bible. Bible teaching permeates every program because we want to know and understand God's Word. The Bible must be lived out in our lives because we believe the Bible is God's Word for what we believe and do. Learning and living the Bible is natural and normal to Wooddale Church.

Outreach-Oriented

Wooddale Church looks outward to serve non-Christians and the unchurched in order to reach them for Jesus Christ. This is woven into everything we do. Outreach orientation requires awareness of our culture and connecting to people as they are and where they are. When a choice is made between serving needs on the inside or reaching out to others, we are committed in advance toward ministry to outsiders. This is done to fulfill our purpose to make more disciples for Jesus Christ.

Disciple-Making

Christians are disciples—believers who are learning and changing to be more like Jesus. Disciple-making is happening when Wooddalers live

Christianly, especially under stress, and especially in demonstrating Christian love in relationships with others. Wooddale Church is a university for disciple-making—offering courses, networking relationships, providing community, showcasing examples, serving as a laboratory, and offering a context for continuous disciple-making.

We will continually change to get the job done. We will include classes, seminars, retreats, mentoring, counseling, and discipling. When appropriate, we will encourage Christians to take advantage of disciple-making opportunities at other churches or through outside organizations. We are far more interested in developing disciples for Jesus Christ than accumulating members for Wooddale Church. We welcome the opportunity to bless Christians who leave Wooddale Church to make disciples in other churches.

Kingdom-Building

The kingdom of Jesus Christ is far greater than any local church or denomination. It includes loyal followers of Jesus all over the world. We are serious about building the kingdom. We want to give away to other churches many of the blessings God has given to us. This is done by starting new churches, encouraging hurting churches, sharing what we have learned, learning from others, sending missionaries, and much more. We rejoice when churches and Christians outside Wooddale Church prosper and succeed—and we are thrilled when God allows us to have a small part in the great good He is doing for them.

Future-Looking

Vision at Wooddale Church is in the future tense because we are future-looking. We know that faith really pleases God, and faith is always forward. Our faith for the future is generated by trust in Jesus Christ. The vision that is God-centered, Bible-based, outreach-oriented, disciple-making, kingdom-building, and future-looking will supernaturally produce a healthy, growing, faithful church. Wooddale Church is like a nuclear generator powered by God, constantly releasing energy to give power and light in many directions.

Sharing the values is more than voicing the values. Every Wooddaler should be able to say them, but that's not enough. As every Wooddaler commits to our values we will pray, work, give, and do whatever needs to be done in order to turn the values we believe into the experiences we share.

We call people to Jesus Christ and the values rather than enrolling members, recruiting teachers, or raising money. Those who share the values will want to join. Those who want to make more disciples will be glad to serve. And, money will follow the values. Frankly, most of us would rather join a movement than a membership list, work for a cause rather than sign up for a job, and give to a vision rather than a budget.

ATHENS CHURCH, ATHENS, GEORGIA

Athens Church is in strategic partnership with North Point Ministries in Alpharetta, Georgia.

As an organization, we are choosing to value these as we pursue our mission:

Biblical Authority: God has spoken to us through the Bible and we recognize it as the final authority for our lives. Are your priorities consistent with Scripture?

Intimacy with God: God desires an intimate relationship with each of us. Is your relationship with God growing?

Relevant Environments: Every environment should be designed to effectively connect with its target audience. Are your environments appealing, engaging, and helpful?

Relational Evangelism: God's message of forgiveness through Christ is most effectively conveyed within the context of personal relationships.

Authentic Community: Accountability, belonging, care, and spiritual growth happen best with relationally connected believers. Are you in a small group?

Strategic Service: Our spiritual gifts have maximum impact when exercised in support of our strategy. Where are you serving?

Intentional Apprenticing: We are responsible to pass along to others the knowledge, skills, and opportunities that have been entrusted to us. Who are you apprenticing?

MARS HILL, GRANDVILLE, MICHIGAN
Our Shared Value

We, as a Mars Hill community, have committed together to pursue a holistic, scriptural way of life that is summed up in six shared values, which we call "The Directions."

The Directions support our mission to join the God of the oppressed. We encourage you to explore all six of the Directions and hope that this will lead you to join in <u>Covenant</u> with the Mars Hill community.

Roots

We affirm the central truths of historic orthodox Christian faith, seeing ourselves in a long line of generations taking part in the endless conversation between God and people. We believe the Bible to be the voices of many who have come before us, inspired by God to pass along their poems, stories, accounts, and letters of response and relationship with each other and the living God. To know where we're going we have to know where we've been.

Journey

We have great confidence that God will restore all of creation under the authority of Christ. We believe that every church has to ask the question, *What does it look like for us to live out that future reality today?* We are constantly exploring, questioning, and wrestling with new and creative ways to live out and communicate the teachings of Jesus. Because we see faith as a journey, change is assumed, innovation is expected, and rebirth is welcomed.

Wholeness

We believe that God wants to bring about a new humanity by redeeming every part of us. We embrace the salvation Jesus offers as the only hope for the healing of our relationships with God, each other, ourselves, and creation. We believe that all of life is spiritual, and that all of our fears, failures, and brokenness can be restored and made whole. We value the inner journey, because we want to be fully integrated people—mind, body, and soul, emotions, and experiences all offered together to God.

Community

We value the image of God in all people, everywhere. We believe that we were created to live deeply with one another, carrying each other's burdens, sharing our possessions, to pray for and confess our sins to each other, to suffer and celebrate together. It's in these honest, loving relationships that God transforms us and truth becomes a reality. The way of Jesus cannot be lived alone.

Serving

We believe that Jesus is God in human form and that the church is God's ongoing presence in the world. Led by the Spirit of God, we are passionate about relieving suffering and fighting injustice, joining the God of the oppressed in living out the transforming message of the resurrected Jesus. Jesus calls his church to be a compelling force for good in the world, and we believe that the church is at its best when it serves, sacrifices, and loves, caring about the things God cares about. We were created to live for something larger than ourselves.

Celebration

We take great joy in partnering with God to change the world, embracing the truth that all of life is sacred, hope is real, and tomorrow can be better than today. We celebrate the divine in the daily, pursuing lives of hope, gratitude, and worship. God invites everyone everywhere into this way of life, and we believe it is the best possible way to live.

Appendix C

Personal Core Values Audit

Directions: Using the scale below, circle the number that best expresses to what extent the following values are important to you (actual values). Work your way through the list quickly, going with your first impression.

1	2	3	4
Not Important	*Somewhat Important*	*Important*	*Very Important*

1. **Family:** *People immediately related to one another by marriage or birth*
   1 2 3 4

2. **Bible knowledge:** *A familiarity with the truths of Scripture*
   1 2 3 4

3. **World missions:** *Spreading the gospel of Christ around the globe*
   1 2 3 4

4. **Encouragement:** *Giving hope to people who need some hope*
   1 2 3 4

5. **Giving:** *Providing a portion of one's finances to support the ministry*
   1 2 3 4

6. **Fellowship:** *Relating to and spending time with others primarily within the church*
   1 2 3 4

7. **Leadership:** A person's ability to influence others to pursue God's mission for the church
1 2 3 4

8. **Cultural relevance:** Communicating truth in a way that people who aren't like us understand it
1 2 3 4

9. **Prayer:** Communicating with God
1 2 3 4

10. **Excellence:** Maintaining the highest of ministry standards that brings glory to God
1 2 3 4

11. **Evangelism:** Telling others the good news about Christ
1 2 3 4

12. **Team ministry:** A group of people ministering together
1 2 3 4

13. **Creativity:** Coming up with new ideas and ways of doing ministry
1 2 3 4

14. **Worship:** Attributing worth to God   1 2 3 4

15. **Cooperation:** The act of working together in the service of the Savior
1 2 3 4

16. **Ministry:** Christians actively involved and serving in the ministries of the church (a mobilized congregation)
1 2 3 4

17. **Obedience:** A willingness to do what God or others ask of a person
1 2 3 4

18. **Innovation:** Making changes that promote the ministry as it serves Christ
1 2 3 4

19. **Initiative:** *The willingness to take the first step or make the first move in a ministry situation*
    1   2   3   4

20. **Community:** *The desire to reach out to the people who live within driving distance of the church (your Jerusalem)*
    1   2   3   4

21. *Other values:*

Note all the values that you rated with a 3 or 4. Rank these according to priority. The first six are your core values.

Appendix D

Church Ministry Core Values Audit

Directions: Using the scale below, circle the number that best expresses to what extent the following values are important to your ministries (actual values). Work your way through the list quickly, going with your first impression.

1	2	3	4
Not Important	Somewhat Important	Important	Very Important

1. **Family:** People immediately related to one another by marriage or birth
   1 2 3 4

2. **Bible knowledge:** A familiarity with the truths of Scripture
   1 2 3 4

3. **World missions:** Spreading the gospel of Christ around the globe
   1 2 3 4

4. **Encouragement:** Giving hope to people who need some hope
   1 2 3 4

5. **Giving:** Providing a portion of one's finances to support the ministry
   1 2 3 4

6. **Fellowship:** Relating to and spending time with others primarily within the church
   1 2 3 4

7. **Leadership:** *A person's ability to influence others to pursue God's mission for the church*
   1   2   3   4

8. **Cultural relevance:** *Communicating truth in a way that people who aren't like us understand it*
   1   2   3   4

9. **Prayer:** *Communicating with God*
   1   2   3   4

10. **Excellence:** *Maintaining the highest of ministry standards that brings glory to God*
    1   2   3   4

11. **Evangelism:** *Telling others the good news about Christ*
    1   2   3   4

12. **Team ministry:** *A group of people ministering together*
    1   2   3   4

13. **Creativity:** *Coming up with new ideas and ways of doing ministry*
    1   2   3   4

14. **Worship:** *Attributing worth to God*
    1   2   3   4

15. **Cooperation:** *The act of working together in the service of the Savior*
    1   2   3   4

16. **Ministry:** *Christians actively involved and serving in the ministries of the church (a mobilized congregation)*
    1   2   3   4

17. **Obedience:** *A willingness to do what God or others ask of a person*
    1   2   3   4

18. **Innovation:** *Making changes that promote the ministry as it serves Christ*
    1 2 3 4

19. **Initiative:** *The willingness to take the first step or make the first move in a ministry situation*
    1 2 3 4

20. **Community:** *The desire to reach out to the people who live within driving distance of the church (your Jerusalem)*
    1 2 3 4

21. *Other values:*

Note all the values that you rated with a 3 or 4. Rank these according to priority. The first six are the church ministry core values.

Appendix E

Mission Development Process

Step 1: Determine what you're supposed to be doing according to the Scriptures.

    1. Are you involved in a church or parachurch ministry?

    2. Whom are you attempting to serve?

    3. How will you minister to people?

Step 2: Articulate your mission in a written statement.

    1. What words communicate best with your people?

    2. Do your people understand what you've written?

    3. Does your mission format convey your mission statement well?

The mission of _____ is to

_____.

Our mission is to _____

_____.

_____ seeks to

_____.

1. Some helpful infinitives.

to assist	to develop	to establish	to produce
to convert	to empower	to help	to promote
to craft	to energize	to lead	to provide
to create	to equip	to prepare	to share

Step 3: Strike a balance between breadth and clarity.

1. Is your mission statement broad enough?
2. Is your mission statement clear?

Step 4: Keep it brief and simple.

1. Have you committed information overload?
2. Does your statement pass the T-shirt test?
3. Can you express your mission in one sentence?
4. Is your mission easily remembered?

Appendix F

Vision Audit

Directions: Read each statement and circle the letter that best represents your preference in a ministry or work-related environment.

1. I tend to
   (a) dislike new problems
   (b) like new problems
2. I work best with
   (a) facts
   (b) ideas
3. I like to think about
   (a) what is
   (b) what could be
4. I like
   (a) established ways to do things
   (b) new ways to do things
5. I enjoy skills that
   (a) I have already learned and used
   (b) are newly learned but unused

6 In my work I tend to
   (a) take time to be precise
   (b) dislike taking time to be precise

7. I would describe my work style as
   (a) steady with realistic expectations
   (b) periodic with bursts of enthusiasm

8. I have found that I am
   (a) patient with routine details
   (b) impatient with routine details

9. I am more likely to trust my
   (a) experiences
   (b) inspirations

10. I am convinced that
    (a) seeing is believing
    (b) believing is seeing

Interpretation: All of the (a) responses are characteristic of nonvisionaries. All of the (b) responses are characteristic of visionaries. If you circled more *a*s than *b*s, then you are a practical realist. If more *b*s than *a*s, then you are a visionary.

notes

INTRODUCTION

1. Randy Frazee with Lyle Schaller, *The Comeback Congregation* (Nashville: Abingdon, 1995), 11.

CHAPTER 1: THE DEFINITION OF CORE VALUES

1. Lynne Hybels and Bill Hybels, *Rediscovering Church* (Grand Rapids: Zondervan, 1995), 153.

2. James M. Kouzes and Barry Z. Posner, *The Leadership Challenge* (San Francisco: Jossey-Bass, 1987), 193.

CHAPTER 2: THE DISCOVERY OF CORE VALUES

1. For a more extensive list of potential values, see the various credos in the appendixes of my book *Values-Driven Leadership: Discovering and Developing Your Core Values for Ministry*, 2nd ed. (Grand Rapids: Baker, 2004).

CHAPTER 3: THE DEVELOPMENT OF CORE VALUES

1. James C. Collins and William C. Lazier, *Beyond Entrepreneurship: Turning Your Business into an Enduring Great Company* (Englewood Cliffs, NJ: Prentice Hall, 1992), 66.

2. "Opening Session Features Ken Blanchard at Wooddale Church," *Compass* 3, no. 3 (February 1994): 1.

3. James C. Collins and Jerry I. Porras, *Built to Last* (New York: Harper Business, 1994), 219.

CHAPTER 4: THE DEFINITION OF MISSION

1. Randy Frazee with Lyle E. Schaller, *The Comeback Congregation* (Nashville: Abingdon, 1995), 6.
2. Peter Drucker, "The New Models," *NEXT* 1, no. 2 (August 1995): 2.
3. Michael Gerber, *The E-Myth* (New York: Harper Business, 1986), 85.

CHAPTER 5: THE DEVELOPMENT OF A MISSION

1. See chapter 4 in my book *Developing a Vision for Ministry in the Twenty-first Century* (Grand Rapids: Baker, 1992).

CHAPTER 6: THE DEFINITION OF VISION, PART 1

1. David L. Goetz, "Forced Out," *Leadership* 17 (Winter 1996): 42.
2. George Barna, "The Man Who Brought Marketing to Church," *Leadership* 16 (Summer 1995): 125.
3. Haddon Robinson, foreword to *Developing a Vision for Ministry in the Twenty-first Century*, by Aubrey Malphurs (Grand Rapids: Baker, 1992), 9–10.
4. Randy Frazee and Lyle Schaller, *The Comeback Congregation* (Nashville: Abingdon, 1995), 11.
5. Ken Hemphill, *Southwestern News*, November/December 1994.

CHAPTER 8: THE DEVELOPMENT OF A VISION

1. Most counseling centers can administer this test.
2. David Kiersey and Marilyn Bates, *Please Understand Me* (Del Mar, CA: Prometheus Nemesis Book Co., 1978), 5–12.
3. Martin Luther King Jr., "I Have a Dream," in *The Words of Martin Luther King, Jr.*, ed. C. S. Kind (New York: Newmarket Press, 1983), 95–98.

4. Rick Warren, *The Purpose Driven Church* (Grand Rapids: Zondervan, 1995), 43.

CHAPTER 9: THE DEFINITION OF STRATEGY

1. I would recommend Guy Scaffold, *Strategic Planning for Christian Organizations* (Fayetteville, AR: Accrediting Association of Bible Colleges, 1994). This book primarily deals with planning for Christian schools, colleges, and seminaries, rather than churches.
2. Peter Drucker, *Managing the Non-Profit Organization* (New York: Harper Collins, 1990), 59.
3. Bob Gilliam, "Are Most Churches Intentionally Making Disciples?" Findings from the "Spiritual Journey Evaluation" (March 29, 1995), 1.
4. James F. Engel and H. Wilbert Norton, *What's Gone Wrong with the Harvest?* (Grand Rapids: Zondervan, 1975), 45.

CHAPTER 10: THE DEVELOPMENT OF A STRATEGY

1. See my book *Advanced Strategic Planning*, 2nd ed. (Grand Rapids: Baker, 2005).
2. See my book *Leading Leaders* (Grand Rapids: Baker, 2005).
3. Bill Hybels, *Courageous Leadership* (Grand Rapids: Zondervan, 2002), 98.
4. Aubrey Malphurs and Steve Stroope, *Money Matters in Church* (Grand Rapids: Baker, 2006).

Index